THE ECONOMIC REVOLUTION

Introducing the creative energy organisation

AuthorHouse™ UK Ltd.
500 Avebury Boulevard
Central Milton Keynes, MK9 2BE
www.authorhouse.co.uk
Phone: 08001974150

First published by AuthorHouse 01/05/2010
ISBN: 978-1-4490-5941-5 (sc)

Copy editor: Lola Oduwole | Translation: Valerie Carroll | Art Direction: www.chocoweb.be

Introduction
Nothing but Voltaire

It is very hard to open a current metaphysical or scientific work without noticing that we live in an era where the partitions of pigeon-hole thinking are disintegrating. Gradually, every type of science interacts with another. Apparent laymen from one field are spreading their ideas and inspiration onto the other. Hawking studies the laws of time and space and arrives at theses which, not so long ago, were rooted in the realms of fantasy novels. The creators of the string theory are opening the perspective towards a multi-dimensional world image, which until quite recently could only be given a platform in religious or philosophical tracts. And the Dalai Lama is writing intriguing books in which he connects quantum physics to the centuries-old insights within his convictions of faith. These are just a few examples of the trend towards the openness between the different areas of specialisation that are creating new insights into human nature and its world. This includes the laws that determine and drive our evolution.

It is precisely because of this cross-disciplinary thinking that the thesis concerning creative energy has also come into being. Whether this book is of a sociological, economic, metaphysical, psychological, ethical, spiritual, mathematical or other nature, remains to be seen. It has simply evolved out of a genuine attempt to give a large number of available facts a more meaningful interpretation. Or, at least, one which is specifically relevant to the era we are now entering.

All of the discoveries concerning creative energy we have presented in this book, which initially conjure up images of advanced mental gymnastics, have been tried and tested in the business world. In this field, we are active as communications advisers, and we use it as our laboratory. Thus, we consider the real pioneers to be the CEOs who kindly permitted us to try out our insights to cultivate their creative energy. Bravely, they were courageous enough to think outside the box and were successful. Creative energy has proven to be a tangible source of vigour, which companies and organisations can tap into in order to be successful in a sustainable and value-added way. It fits with the evolving mindset and the social and economic challenges we face.

It is a privilege to be afforded the time and space to think about tomorrow's new order. We are living in a new era of enlightenment, in which we can all feel a touch of Voltaire. This is also why we are advocating that you, as one of the liberal thinkers of our time and as visionary CEOs, read this book. Explore with us, new concepts, about the dynamics of creativity, of living and working together and help to shape what is just around the corner. Join us in the pursuit of new insights, which can make tomorrow's society and economy evolve in an optimal way, successful for everyone, without taboos and applying straightforward and pragmatic thinking. Ultimately, you will be one of those who gathers inspiration from around you and delivers results to the world.

Good luck / Art Kristeven

Part 1

towards new paradigms

or how, in the community context, we need new ways of living and working together

Chapter **one** To evolve or not to evolve, that's the question

In a word

It is inherent in the genes of each individual to grow and evolve. In order to make our evolution manageable we adopt concept frameworks. These are the generally accepted truths on which we shape and structure our reality. They are also called paradigms. Nevertheless, from time to time man's evolution extends outside the existing framework. This is the moment when a new truth needs to be created as a new platform for continued evolution.

Since the beginning of time people have had an instinct for growth and evolution. Our life is an evolution. You're born, grow, establish a life for yourself and it is assumed, that through experience, you become ever wiser. At any given moment in time, we constantly challenge ourselves and our fellow beings to achieve more than we believe we are capable of. We are genetically compelled to make progress, to visualize both the past and what is yet to come. We are compelled to continually make our own potential tangible and that of our peers and we do this because evolution gives each individual and every group an enhanced sense of existence, self-esteem and success.

🔊 *"It is inherent in human nature to grow and evolve. We are genetically compelled to make progress, to visualize both what has been and what is yet to be discovered. We feel compelled to continually make our own potential tangible and that of our peers."*

This is reflected in every aspect of our of daily behaviour: wherever one is active, makes an effort or undertakes a commitment, he or she derives a sense of pleasure from the idea of having 'achieved' something, however large or small the task. From 'I'm capable of mowing my lawn perfectly symmetrically and I'll show you' to 'I've made an essential contribution to the development of a linear accelerator, a globally-important development.' This concept also applies to areas where people collaborate. In companies and organisations this translates in concrete terms as: evolution and success linked to attaining concrete goals.

There is nothing we enjoy more than demonstrating our potential to ourselves and to the rest of the world. But what are the limits to this development? Do we never collide with an invisible, but certainly existent, upper limit to our ability? Is what is implicitly contained in our potential so infinite, that our growth is ongoing, evolves, and we constantly surpass ourselves? It certainly seems that way. Growth never stops. History reveals the improbable flexibility that exists in relation to everything that is intrinsic to mankind. This applies individually and collectively, intellectually, emotionally, physically and on many other known and unknown levels, where we function both consciously and subconsciously. We learnt to think, communicate, walk and run, make tools and develop machines. We created insight into our own body, in the laws of nature and various religious entities. We learnt to buy and sell, developed both a physical and emotional sense of value. We tried to organise and then re-organise ourselves, to enable us to live and work together within a consensus structure. To sum up, we achieved with our intellect, time and again, more than we could ever have imagined in our wildest dreams.

Each step in our history is characterised by a number of paradigms. They relate to concept frameworks, which are accepted during a certain period as the most accurate and precise way of describing the pattern of life and community on earth, at that particular time. They reflect the boundaries of our capacity for understanding and the domain of unknown possibilities within it. To make an analogy, imagine all of this as a fish bowl where the distance we are able to swim is governed by what we know. In this sense, this paradigm illustrates the playing field for the era in which we now live. It sets out the consensus of what we know and provides a basis for continued growth and evolution.

"Paradigms are concept frameworks which are accepted during a certain period in our history as the most accurate and precise way of describing the patterns of life on earth at that particular time."

PARADIGMS: ILLUSTRATE THE PLAYING FIELD OF THE ERA

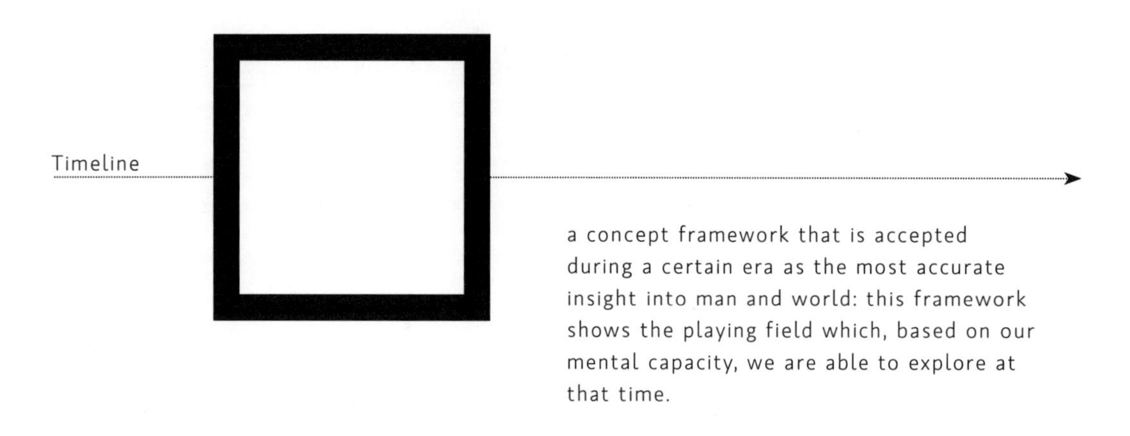

It is clear that there comes a certain point, when man's growth and evolution, enclosed within the existing consensus, is realised. It is precisely at this moment that man collides with the limitations of his own understanding. Indeed, he evolves constantly and makes his way in the real world where his growth can no longer be supported by the prevailing concept framework. These are moments when problems and questions can no longer be resolved with the paradigms indicative of the scope inherent in the era. A new pathway into the laws of life and coexistence is required, something that is more relevant, broader and robust. Man is then confronted by the challenge to expand his understanding and to identify more precisely the trends in his evolution and in the world at large. When he succeeds in this, he reaches a turning point. We are embarking on a new era in which one is able to discover new possibilities and address new potential based on a broader understanding of oneself and the world.

Voltaire's enlightened concepts, Newton's apple or Bacon's empiricism: these are but a few examples of the brilliant visionary insights which surpassed the limitations of an era in order to clear the way for a multitude of new possibilities. In this way, man leaps from era to era, each time moving from the fish bowl of the moment and diving into a bigger pool of possibilities. We clarify this law through a thought experiment.

🔊 *"At a certain point there comes a turning point. A moment where we are in a position to expand our understanding and to better identify the trends of our own evolution and of the world at large."*

Experiment 1: the finite garden

Suppose that person A lives on a huge piece of land in isolation and has never travelled anywhere else nor met anyone. His overview of the area extends as far as a dense line of trees. Seen from his perspective, it would be true to say that the world in which he lives stretches as far as he can see; namely, the dense row of trees. It is a perfectly legitimate concept framework within which he can experience all that is possible. Now, imagine that after a while, he walks towards the row of trees and notices that, behind the dense wall of trunks, there is a new similar piece of land, again bordered by trees. This experience exceeded his original concept. Beyond his world, there is another that perhaps offers new possibilities for development and evolution. And beyond the row of trees of this second world, perhaps there exists yet another. His encounter means that the image of the world for him, has now changed and he is compelled to adopt a new one. Clearly, it is now more accurate to say that the world extends much further than he had envisaged.

Is it possible that we are now also living in the turning-point phase, which gives us a feeling of being limited by current truths? An era in which we, as individuals and with our society, are hungry for new possibilities, new reference points in order to be able to handle the evolution which we ourselves have unleashed? Are we looking in the fish bowl of this era for the impetus which will propel us into the next evolutionary leap? The fact is that paradoxes drawn up by the era in which we now live, make it clear that our evolution can no longer be supported or explained by yesterday's concepts. A new and broader concept framework looms in the distance.

PARADIGM CHANGE: BROADENING OF CONCEPTUAL FRAMEWORK

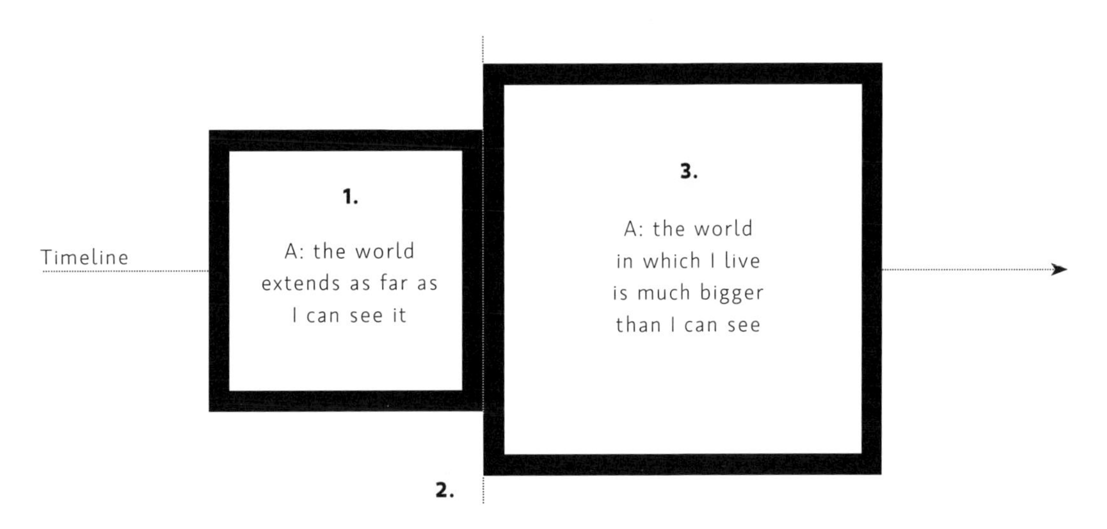

1. As time progresses, A develops in his finite world
2. A's evolution reaches as far as the border of his world and then beyond it he discovers a new similar area
3. A broadens his conceptual framework, from where he can discover new things and evolve further

Chapter **two** Where is our world?

In a word

A number of societal tendencies are revealed in an important paradox, which is occurs due to a change of attitude of the individual towards his surroundings. In the past, the context in which we lived gave us an attainable, understandable and safe environment. It seems that this time has passed and that we need to design new models for living together, that give us the capacity to further our societal development.

The concept framework, which at this point has resulted in an evolutionary paradox, relates to the relationship between the individual and his environment. It seems as if the conventions that supplied us with a more or less safe structure in which we could live and work, are now faltering. The tremendous speed with which we have rocketed forward on the technological and scientific front has indeed made the world in which we live more accessible, but mentally and emotionally it is perceived as increasingly impervious, less comprehensible and unsafe. Interestingly, this evolution also implies that new insights and opportunities will emerge. Three major trends during the last decades illustrate this trend.

Broadening of one's environment: freedom vs. powerlessness

Up until quite recently, one's area of activity was close to home. We lived in a structure that was within reach and familiar. It provided a clearly defined field of reference for our development. In the meantime, our personal environment has expanded exponentially and, whether we like it or not, we suffer the consequences of global citizenship. The scope of economic, financial and technological power centres throughout the continents has become so enormous that this scaling-up has powerfully impacted every individual's life, on all fronts. As a result, companies increasingly operate in a transnational and multinational framework. Decisions affecting each of us are taken at a level that is outside of our control. The boss who once hired or fired you still had a recognizable face. Now, factories in one continent close down because of decisions made in another. This evolution has given us the feeling that we, as individuals, are losing our grip on our surroundings. The more globally the world functions, the more impenetrable it seems to be for each individual.

🔊 *"We find ourselves as participants in a spatial paradox which triggers our search for new boundaries and structures."*

On the other hand, the potential is now literally stirring up unlimited personal development. The entire globe now appears as a playing field where it seems every individual initiative is virtually attainable. As a result, we feel freer but less empowered. We are participants in a spatial paradox that triggers our search for new boundaries and structures.

Accessibility of information: ambiguity vs. comprehension

Today, in whatever environment we are involved, in both our professional and private lives, we are inundated with visual, auditory, emotional and mental stimuli. The most diverse channels overwhelm us with different 'truths'. What you read in one newspaper as a consumer is contradicted in a news announcement. When a company announces, through its local communications campaign, that it is stable, the next day that is superseded by a different information channel that a branch in a different country faces closure. We are informed about everything. It is assured by the unceasing and pervasive multi-media information, which inundates us each and every day. As a result, every stance, each point of view, every objective proposition can be quickly modified by new information or an opinion formed from a different perspective. Solid truth no longer exists. Knowledge is more than ever before, a living concept that is barely manageable since every 'objective fact' which confronts us can, rightly or wrongly, also be nullified.

We are entangled in a paradox where, on the one hand, the input of information and perceptions leads to confusion and ambiguity, but in contrast they offer the perfect opportunity to obtain a more accurate understanding of reality. Our environment no longer determines what is true, we have the authority to create our own perspective on the world.

Can the information flow be managed?

Attempts to manage the information stream are steadily becoming less efficient, thereby impacting the perception of what is true. It would require a type of monitoring that is no longer available. Nevertheless, on every continent you still see attempts being made to weave in political or economic structures that try to convince people of a single clear-cut truth by endeavouring to censure or manage the media. Those concerned undertake the task with inadequate force, imagining they can retain yesterday's status quo. Information is constantly becoming less manageable, so that what is communicated still filters through to every citizen or consumer.

Financial crisis: prosperity vs. welfare

In considering all aspects, we live in a world where we have scrutinized the boundaries of our image of our consumption-driven society. After the industrial revolution, we opted for a state of prosperity, where the prime aim of work was to improve people's prosperity not their welfare. Our society became based on the monetary structures we had built. It was the pursuit of having more that constantly drove the world forward and made everyone believe in financial castles in the sky. Stock markets where money is traded like air have had to be rescued by governments to pre-empt their later being confronted with a mountain of debt pulling them to the edge of insolvency. The property markets have all but collapsed, interest rates have fallen, people and companies have gone bankrupt. In short: the financial structures on which our belief system for prosperity is based, have reached their limits.

It is as though we are awakening from a fiction and see that we are living in a world where our need for welfare is not satisfied by the pursuit of prosperity, because it can no longer provide this. We note that the socio-economic framework, which for a long time offered security, is no longer able to deliver what we want.

Yet we must not make the mistake of hiding behind a scapegoat. It is all too easy to saddle the blame on politics, high finance or other representatives within our society and make them carry the can for the problems of our time. The custodians of true power, in our time, is a balance between those who determine purchasing power and those who seek it. In truth, it is not only the bankers and major exchanges who call the shots but so does the individual.

To think about considering new financial structures is like kicking in an open door. It is clear that, inherent in the current malaise, we have the potential to evolve towards a radically modified system of value transfer. The impulse for this stems from the fact that we cannot only express value in rigid monetary terms.

"It is as though we are awakening from a fiction and see that we are living in a world in which the contrast between prosperity and welfare is both more visible and larger. Each individual realises the cold reality that the social framework which had formerly provided security, is suddenly no longer satisfactory."

These tendencies make it clear that we have grown out of the safe classical relationship with the world around us. Our environment no longer provides the reference point, concept and prosperity it formerly held. We're on our own. The paradox is that on the one hand this triggers confusion, but on the other it inspires us with the opportunity to take more responsibility for our personal and collective evolution. When we analyze this in greater depth, we create a new concept framework that offers us the possibility to unearth inherent dormant potential and discover other options.

The awareness revolution

This changing social context is no transient hype analysis. After the industrial and technical revolutions, it is time for the awareness revolution. In the last few centuries, we have expanded and developed our world at an incredible pace. In all areas of our lives, social, economic and especially technical-industrial we have progressed in leaps and bounds, and we still continue to develop. Developers today work their fingers to the bone to ensure continued world progress. In essence, while we are able to clone ourselves ... We still feel smaller, more fragile and more threatened than ever. We are the cause of a trend that we do not seem to be able to control. Progress moves so quickly that our collective understanding can hardly keep pace. It seems that it has arrived at a standstill in the thunderous rhythm of new possibilities. Therefore, it is hugely important to see how, together, we can escape this fish bowl of our undoubtedly still limited understanding and dive into a collaboratively ocean of new wisdom to develop a collective awareness that enables us to manage the speed and power with which mankind grows.

Chapter **three** The truth becomes 'my' truth

In a word

Nowadays, the individual ranks himself above his environment for evolution. His behaviour is shaped from his own feelings, experiences and beliefs, and not on the rational framework created by his surroundings. This causes a chaos that falls away when we develop an evolutionary methodology that involves the integration of a ratio of feelings and the human being and the world in which he is active.

A logical reaction in an era when mankind experiences significantly less clarity, structure and safety, is to withdraw within oneself. In the past, where he might have used the rational structured environment as a benchmark to determine his behaviour, he now uses his own emotion. The individual frame of reference becomes the new norm. To clarify the implications of this evolution precisely, it's worth taking a brief look at human behavioural psychology.

People are life's 'hands-on' experts. In each phase of life and in every setting, we acquire experience from which we learn and evolve. And everything we experience we store consciously, but especially subconsciously. The more drastic the experience, the more powerfully it is ingrained into our system. On this basis, we develop personal convictions and this shapes our attitude to the world. For instance, someone who, in their opinion, has been fired three times consecutively in an offensive way, is likely to be convinced that employers are unreliable and thus adopt a distrustful attitude towards future employers. Similarly, someone who has been brought up in an authoritarian environment will view people in power differently from someone who has been raised in a more relaxed style. Each individual will devise their own unique set of values and norms based on their life experiences. To a large extent, this occurs subconsciously and is expressed, quite simply, in the behaviour itself. This makes perfect sense since it relates to the motivation imprinted by experience.

In the past, we were more focused on the power of reason. The unprecedented flexibility of our intellect led us to discover and rediscover, but at the same time our entire world, including the realm of emotion, was very cerebral. A rational explanation or interpretation was found for everything. Happiness became success. Welfare became prosperity. This evolution is evident from the way that we organised ourselves. Structures where people came together, such as companies, streamlined individual behaviour from a rational consensus. Concrete rules, values and norms were agreed with the aim of enabling everything to run as smoothly and efficiently as possible. Being part of a broader framework automatically implied subscribing to this behavioural consensus with the aim of shared achievement and development. The environment was the benchmark for the cohesion of human behaviour. The initiative, and especially the responsibility for progress was rooted in the broader structure of which one was a part.

EARLIER:
RATIONAL ENVIRONMENT
STANDARDISES BEHAVIOUR

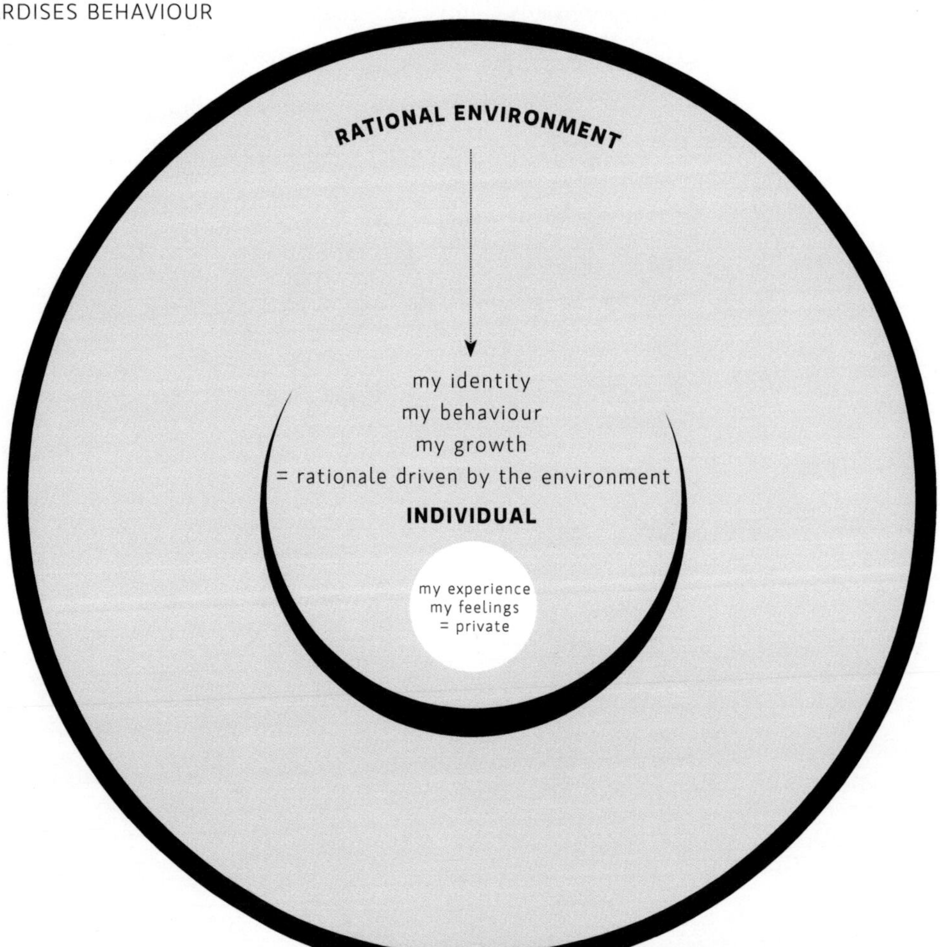

RATIONAL ENVIRONMENT

my identity
my behaviour
my growth
= rationale driven by the environment

INDIVIDUAL

my experience
my feelings
= private

Values and norms in the world

Values which are accepted in a broad social or professional environment are intended to ensure that the group operates in an ordered, structured and, as a result, productive way. They are converted into a consensus of behaviour. Anyone who deviates from the behaviour that is determined by the group, to a certain degree, can be reprimanded through a social judgement. If, for example, team spirit is shown in a company by having lunch together each day, the employee who does not participate, but is exemplary in every other way, will be less readily accepted by the group. There are also values that are considered to be so important that the linked behaviour is enforced by transforming them into norms. Where values consist of very broad concepts, which can be interpreted differently (freedom, after all, is defined differently from one person to another) the norms assign the boundaries of the behaviour linked to particular values. They function as the 'big stick' required to guarantee the structure: just as in the legal system, where western fundamental values like freedom, equality, justice and universality are translated into specific normalizing rules of behaviour.

It was also considered normal for people to embrace the company values and norms and those of the community in which they lived and worked, as their own truth and to behave accordingly. And it worked. One partially derived one's identity from the broader framework where one was active. Personal feelings and the individual sphere of experience also existed, but it was kept private and often suppressed. The rational framework we stepped into, determined our growth. The dynamics that evolved were the same for the individual as for the environment we lived in. Our personal feelings were mainly considered as a capricious, disbelieving factor that made working and living together unnecessarily complex.

Next step in emancipation?

In the last century, the struggle for emancipation also developed from well-organised and rationalised frameworks. Labourers, women and other groups combined their strengths in robust divisions to give their own identity a strong voice. Very many people drew strength and self-esteem from these powerful networks. A next logical step is that following this collective de-paternalizing, a sustained individual emancipation follows whereby, in addition to the rationale, personal sentiment is also respected. The boom experienced in the last fifty years in psychological support blatantly signals the growing need for personal development and is an indication of the many deadlocked emotions and built-up convictions which have been ignored in society's pent up ideas of truth.

This still persists in the way the structures in which we live and work are organised. However, this is no longer tenable. When a person changes their attitude towards their environment, their personal behaviour will no longer be principally determined by the rational organisation installed by a certain structure. It will instead be formed, much more, by individual emotions and convictions drawn from highly personal life experiences. In the current and future generations everyone will set their own benchmark in life. The result is that 'the truth' will no longer exist but become 'my truth', the individual subjective framework with its own specific cocktail brewed from highly individual emotions; concept formation and expression becomes the standard. In this way, we jointly create an individual territorial awareness within an expanding environment: an awareness that is gathering momentum. This awareness exists on all levels in our life - as an alert consumer, conscientious employee, informed member or non-member of the electorate. This awareness enables us to deal with a myriad of impulses and truths that bombard us daily from all corners of the globe.

The individual is the reference point for his own behaviour and growth. In other words, he claims the right to initiate the evolution. In this, the evolution dynamic is applied based on subjective emotions, which consequently make known that there are just as many truths and worlds as there are people. Naturally, this clashes with every broader framework that results in the installation of a single enduring world image, within which each individual is expected to behave as prescribed, in order to attain certain goals. This gives rise to explosive situations: the individual feels misunderstood by his environment, but still needs it to evolve. After all, we cannot live in isolation. Everyone needs nurturing experiences to make the next step in their progress. We clarify this evolution based on a thought experiment.

NOW: PERSONAL DYNAMIC STANDARDIZES BEHAVIOUR / CONFRONTATION WITH RATIONAL ENVIRONMENT

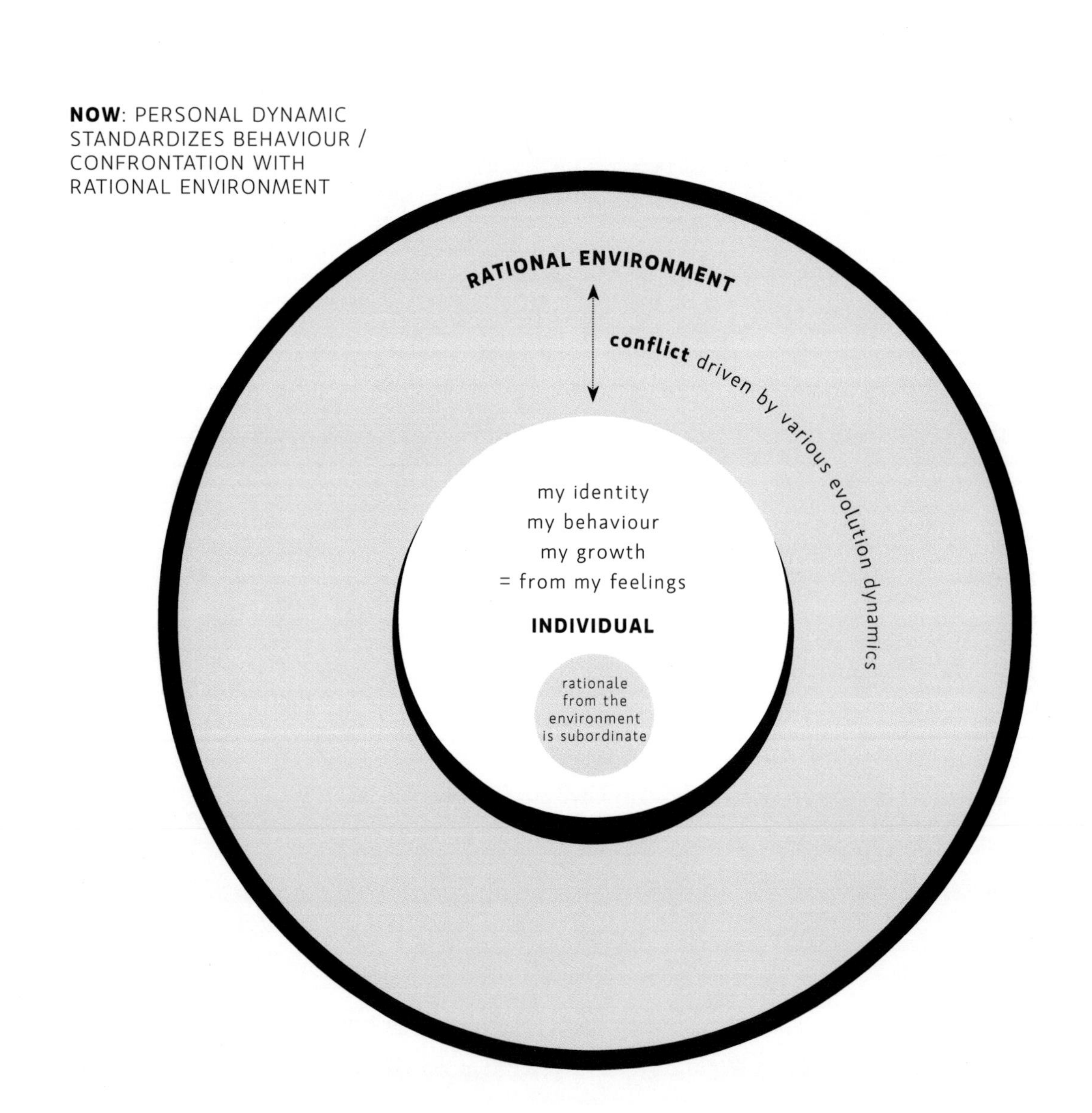

Experiment 2: the relative space

Suppose we create a round flat circle upon which sits a single living creature, who we will call person A, and that we can all observe him from another planet. He exists only by our acknowledgement; the observer. From his perspective, the platform on which he lives exists only in his vision. He gives this a significance and can say, for instance: "This platform is the world."

We then decide to intervene and place person B into this circle. From this moment on, neither A nor B exists through our acknowledgement as the observer, but in relation to each other. They both develop an individual awareness of each other and are able to identify themselves as 'I' and the other as 'you'. In addition, it is no longer possible for A to dictate the plane on which they both function unilaterally. In fact, this space does not exist in terms of one or the other but is the same for the both of them. A, who represents the 'we-awareness' develops a perspective from which the communal space can be described. Together they can decide on the significance they will give to it.

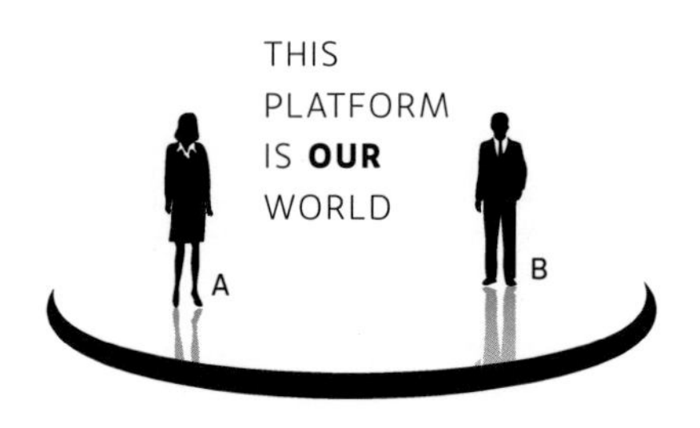

In this thesis, they are in agreement about the significance they place on the space in which they function. The shared space is clearly assigned. On this basis, A and B can undertake further decisions about the way in which they delineate this world.

But precisely because A and B now exist in relation to each other, they are able to express themselves individually. Thus, A could, justifiably say: in my observation this area is small. And B, on the other hand, could contend that, as far as he is concerned, it is actually rather a large area. Both are equally legitimate in reporting their experience. They are still located in the same place but perceive this area in a different way and each of them gives it a different significance. Thus, each from their personally discovered individuality is able to claim the communal physical environment as their world and consequently say: "my world is large" and "my world is small".

It begs the question as to which world A or B actually lives. Can we talk about a communal platform or do they each live in their own world of awareness? Since they place a different significance on the shared space, we can assume that the latter applies. In fact, the space they occupy is not the same for either of them. The communal platform is no longer created from a collectively allocated significance. A and B have created two complete worlds which are unique and personal, and from which they each function entirely separately. Neither A nor B is able to enter the other's world of awareness. When we illustrate these two worlds separately we arrive at a paradox.

It is impossible to imagine presenting two planes that are separated from each other. After all, A and B derive their right of existence and individuality from each other because they are situated together on the same plane. Thus, there can be no suggestion of two different circles. Clearly, they are linked together and their worlds cannot be separated, although at the same time, the worlds are fundamentally different. The platform serves as the reference point that links one to the other and from which they shape their own world. It would be impossible to divide the space into two platforms.

Thus, we are looking to find a new kind of solidarity between the shared platform and the individual worlds of awareness which A and B have developed. The paradox can be solved if we consider the shared space as relative. Both A and B translate the initial platform from the original dynamic in a separate dimension of it. This is presented in the diagram.

In addition to the shared platform, two extra dimensions come into existence if the initial disc were to become a ball. The platform remains in existence as a reference point for A and B but does not determine the significance of the world where they both live. Each of them lives exclusively in their own world, which is an individually created translation of the dimension of the reference platform. The A + B world is thus no longer the same as the platform, but it amounts to a new communal environment: the ball. Compared to the initial platform this is proportionally exponentially enlarged with two extra dimensions.

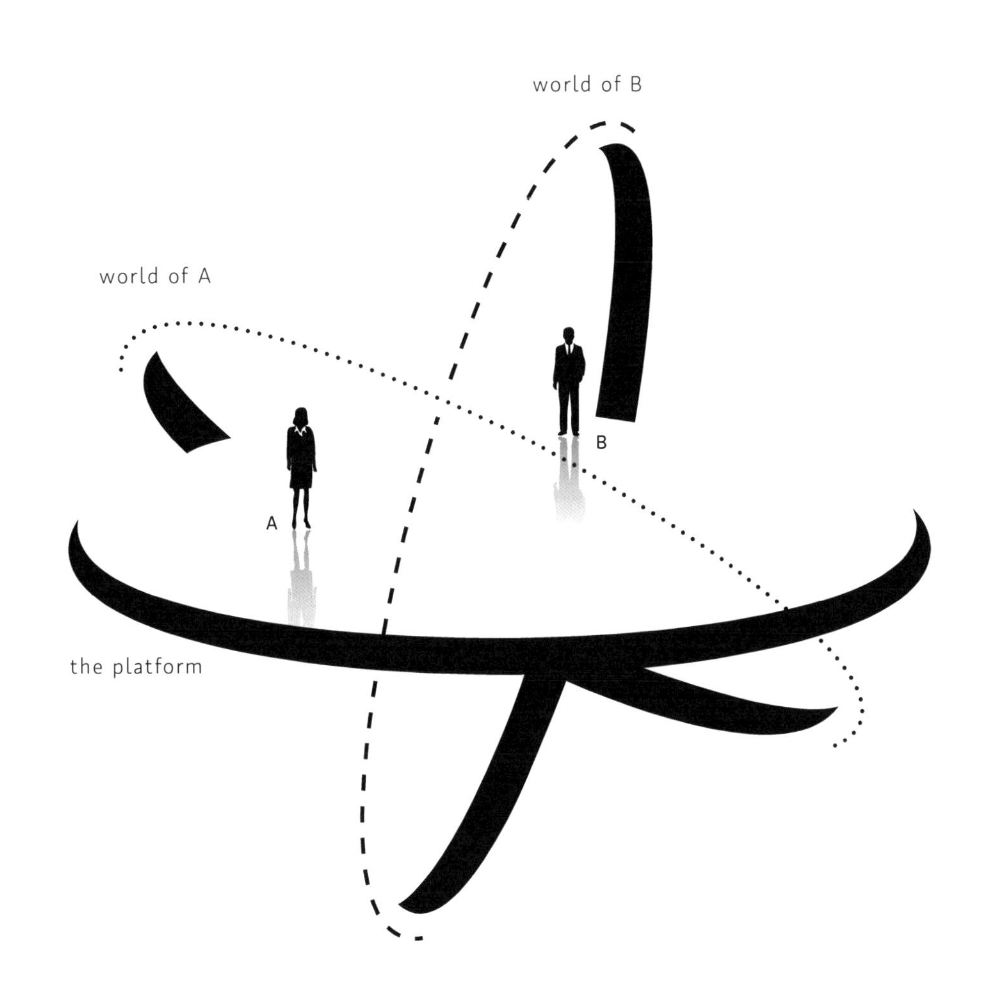
world of B
world of A
B
A
the platform

From now on, the communality between A and B cannot possibly be rooted in a particular agreed conceptual framework. On balance, everyone bases his own concept and paradigms on the norms within his own world. Thus, it is completely justified that one person may consider their world as infinite and the other as finite. Furthermore, each has their own concept of time and space. We can easily conclude that the time and the space no longer exist. There are an equal number of perceptions as there are people, and therefore, worlds. It makes little sense to give space to the time by determining a common paradigm. In other words, the communal platform is no longer a determinant of the significance of the world where one lives, but has evolved to a reference platform for the different individual dimensions of which they are a part.

This experiment teaches us that each environment merits its own significance. When this significance is born of a communal understanding, the existing space remains one-dimensionally demarcated. When the significance is born of various individual perceptions, the shared space becomes relative and additional dimensions of significance come into play thereby expanding it. We can assume that this dimension expansion is equal to the number of individuals who, due to their individual convictions, are part of that space. Each of them claims the entire space as their own and in doing so, creates an extra level of significance. Each individual entry into the environment spawns an extra dimension. The opposite occurs when someone leaves the shared environment. This makes the shared space a constantly changing and evolving environment. This does not determine the individual's direction, but reverses it.

On balance, we can deduce from this that from the moment people function uniquely from their own world of awareness, the environment - and by extension the possibilities and the ensuing exploitable energy, is also increased. When we assume that each individual wants to evolve together with the others, then it is important, in the frame of this increased space, to find new communal patterns, which ensure that these newly created options are fully utilised.

Thus, each person is their world. The truth becomes their truth. It amounts to finding an integrated system in such a multi-dimensional world image, where people arrive at a mutually sustaining behaviour between themselves. And one in which each environment surpasses the proven communal concept frameworks with new ways of living and working together on a personal and communal level.

Object and subject: Bacon and Shakespeare together again

The time is ripe to unify Francis Bacon and William Shakespeare once again. The first of these men encouraged people through experience to observe objectively the patterns of creation. It entailed the start of an unmistakable flowering of inductive thinking that gave our civilization the development speed we know today. Shakespeare then showed the inner subjective world of individual values and life choices. A world of feelings and strong emotions of love, hate, grief and passion. These two contemporaries have thus demonstrated that the objective world is separated from the subjective. The one objective world was that of 'the commonly accepted truth'. The other world was that of the subjective 'I'. The latter could hardly be associated with the 'real' world because the chaos of highly individual emotions would make a workable coexistence impossible. Today, we find that the distinction between these two worlds is no longer clear. Objective observations and subjective experiences are being viewed as equal. The border between these equally valuable worlds is blurred. Tomorrow's truth lies further away than in the purely cerebral empirical consensus. Each individual, emotionally-orientated perception of reality will have to be taken into account.

Viewing it from this perspective, a morally judgemental sense of values, scandalised by the hyper-individualism of this era, is irrelevant. It is nothing more than a logical step in our development, but one that has significant consequences. Each broader structure will be obliged to assume an organisational dynamic which accredits each individual in their own pursuit towards stronger personal awareness. This implies that the environment must strive to determine the action (behaviour) not only from the thought process (rational structure) but also recognising the emotion (personal dimension). 'What I feel is the truth: not what my surroundings tell me' is tomorrow's adage. This is why each 'external' truth will be assessed through one's own intuition. When these do not match up, the individual will make choices and apply themselves with less drive, panache and satisfaction to the larger entity. In a nutshell, individual feelings and perceptions demand acknowledgement within our societal structure, alongside the strongly cerebral world, which we have developed over the centuries.

This applies to the economy, politics, our legal system, education and also to the business world.

We all need to bear the consequences of the fact that we all want a piece of the pie, to share the evolution. It offers us the responsibility to challenge ourselves in our personal growth in the environment, which has granted recognition. By constantly encountering new experiences, we will be in a position to expand our awareness. Through drafting our own pool of convictions, based on the understanding of another's equally important truth, our world becomes increasingly richer, wider and more nuanced. This will lead to our ongoing joint creation of a powerful expansion, which will draw out the maximum potential for living and working together. As a result, we will be able to develop a broader and improved appreciation, enabling us to move a step further, both jointly and individually. Our growing self-awareness will ensure that we remain the creator of our own universe.

FUTURE:
INDIVIDUAL AND ENVIRONMENT DRIVE INTEGRATED BEHAVIOURAL DYNAMIC

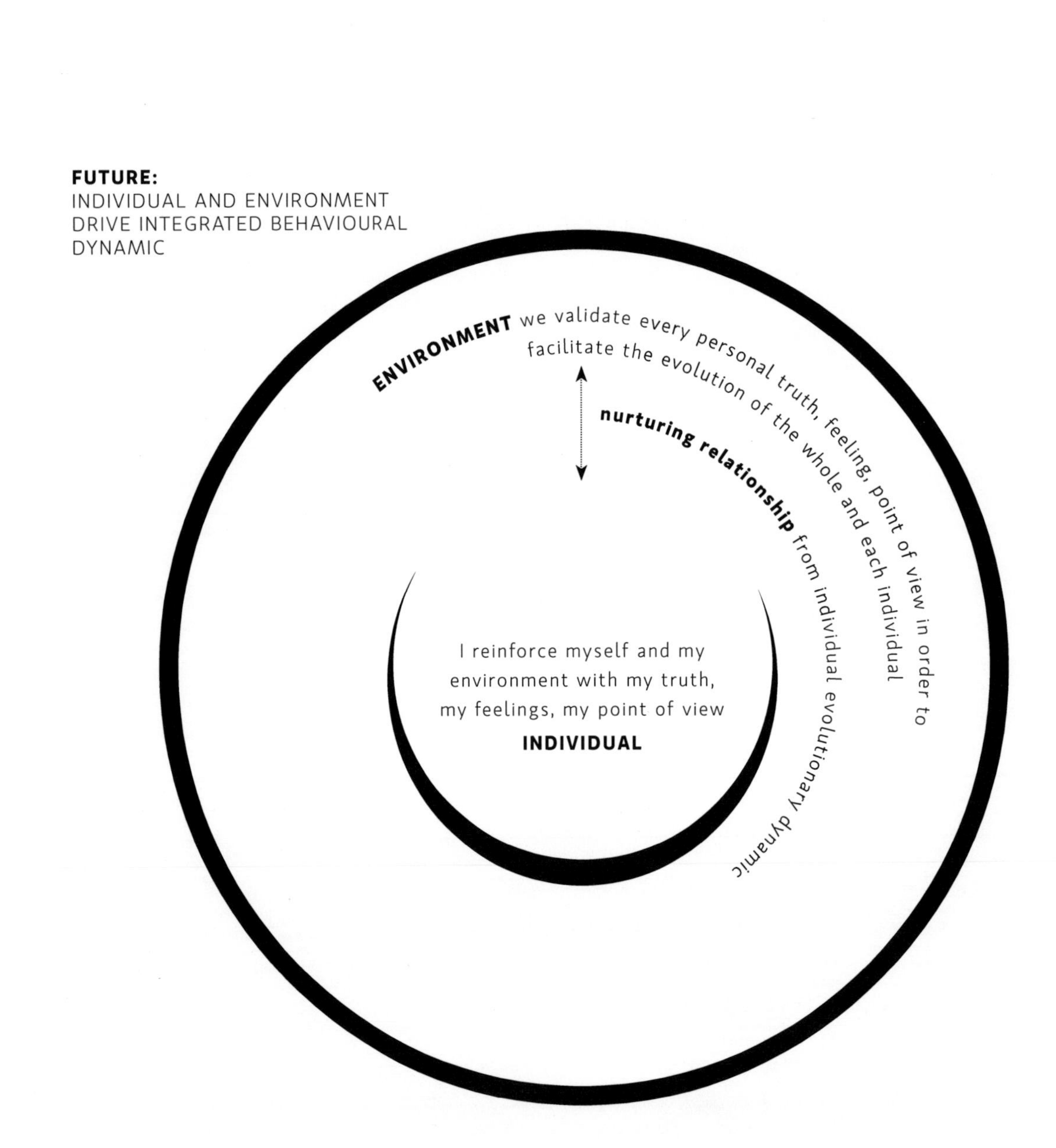

This historical phase is one of transition. Noticeably, people and structures endeavour to advance further towards a new concept of reality that they have created together. And one that is also visible now. It is illustrated in the behaviour people adopt to explore the boundaries of what is feasible when they step into what is otherwise a boundless world. Additionally, it is logical that the more egocentric reflex makes it easier to push beyond our own boundaries and those of our environment. What's more, the social control of yesterday's small environment has dissipated. Gradually, each individual will strongly delineate and mark out the boundaries of their own private environment. This however, heightens the risk of conflict. Clearly, any situation where people come together sparks a colourful mix of small individual worlds and truths.

The next step consists of searching for a new manageable benchmark which can be applied to communal living and working structures where there are opposing forces between the individual and the environment. One in which each individual is able and allowed to live out his own truth, more than ever before. But simultaneously, there is the challenge to expand personal truth and awareness through confronting new experiences in the broader context where one functions. In this kind of framework, the conflict of individual truths will not lead to the debilitating collapse of the larger entity, infecting every member of it, but will lead precisely to a new fusion. The fusion results in energy being generated by groups of people, which we have called 'creative energy'.

I like the one who dreams the impossible (Goethe)

Imagination is a valid, but not immediately obvious tool for conjuring up new sociological patterns, which sketch the future evolution for man and society. With this approach you can access the truth which could apply a hundred years from now. If you refer to our collective history, then you can safely conclude that we created and achieved things that greatly exceeded our imagination. This is why the imagination should be called upon, at the precise moments when you are looking for new options. Imagination is without restraints, and has the power to navigate new truths, permitting people to dream the impossible. It is exactly these dreams that prompted the search for ways of realising them. Goethe was not the only one who understood that. Martin Luther King also opened the door to the inordinate, and at that time, unattainable power of a suppressed section of the population when he said: 'I have a dream'. He articulated their dream - a people who throughout history had been severely mistreated. Forty years later, his dream has been realised and a black president is the incumbent at the White House. That is due in part to the pastor who projected his ideal onto the world. Imagination opens doors to a future, which no-one believes possible.

Part 2

to the core of the business

or how every company can summon its creative energy

Chapter **four** The company as microcosm

In a word

It is in the world of economics that we'd like to look for new workable systems of cooperation. Surely, each company is a microcosm that applies to the described evolution. The human capital is of critical importance for the success of each organisation. In the current strongly subjective contexts, it becomes increasingly difficult to gather people around a common goal. The classic top-down structure is less successful in streamlining human behaviour because it doesn't take into account the benchmark positioned by each individual on the basis of his own emotions.

Social analyses are obviously very interesting, but they only become truly functional when they are applied to systems that assist us in our daily life. We seek out what can help each person and each group of people to evolve into a nourishing, beneficial, prosperous way of living and working in all areas in tomorrow's world.

Understanding creative energy not only provides a theoretical framework to highlight the ongoing paradigm shift, it can also be applied to a clear workable plan that can be used in any developing constellation of human awareness. It can also be employed to establish a social structure at a national, regional or local level. Creative energy can be used to shape political, cultural and economic environments into solid structures for the future. Every person involved can benefit via their own personal evolution.

In the context of this book, we place the focus on the economic domain. The methodology that we offer provides a pathway for business to address the recession and work towards a healthy future. Here, we interpret the term 'business' very broadly, meaning any structure or organisation that employs people. Thus, it is equally applicable to government institutions and NGOs, as undoubtedly there are managers in both, whose mandate it is to ensure a flourishing operation.

We chose the economic organisation and environment for several reasons. First and foremost, this world is the most determinant and yet is also particularly vulnerable in our society. The impact of the installation of a new way of co-operating in this context will therefore result in the best possible outcome for you and me. The critical leverage for the evolution of man and society is located precisely where the powerhouse of the era lies.

Furthermore, our own professional world is one where we give companies advice about their structure, profile and communication strategy. As stated, we have found real sparring partners in very many CEOs and CFOs. They are always driven to search for structural means to maximize their value, and get the best out of the future. What more does a manager want than the success of his organisation? He is permanently striving for the right strategy to extract the best out of his employees and assets, always focused on being better and stronger in the market. To garner more honour and glory for himself, his employees, and with luck, improve their joint remuneration. The understanding that this is not wrong and can be applied in a way where everyone is aligned, is a premise that directly relates to all CEOs since it falls within their responsibilities. This has resulted in a significant number of managers approaching us in recent years and giving us the opportunity of benchmarking the creative energy theory against daily practice.

🔊 *"We chose the business world to appraise our analysis because the world of economics is now the most determinant factor in our society. The critical leverage for the evolution of man and society is located precisely where the powerhouse of the era sits."*

Time and again companies prove to be fascinating microcosms in which the social analysis mentioned above is clearly noticeable, relevant and tangible. Because here too, the individual's behaviour towards the environment is increasingly self-aware and clashes with the classic top-down structure still applied by the majority of companies. On balance, this is aimed at the rational control and management of those active in the organisation. This is experienced as a capping of increasingly important individual feelings. It translates into a personal and often logical attitude by the employees, which generates both suppressed and articulated tensions. We then have an environment where everyone joins the structure based on his own truth and follows his own stated or hidden agenda.

A great deal of useful energy is lost. The unreal world you create by doing this consists of a chaotic collection of individuals who use their own energy for self-preservation not to nurture the whole. Only in this context do they step into unilaterally imposed boundaries. There is little evidence of a group culture and equally, of added value.

Thus, it is clear that it is no longer acceptable to force people in your organisation via a top-down approach into a company straitjacket. The time when the boss made decisions based purely on profit is over. You're no longer dealing with a sheep-like type mentality. Situations like these illustrate the perfect example of the clash between the environment, which in the past was the initiator and responsible for our development, and the individual who gradually takes on the task himself.

THE TOP-DOWN STRUCTURE

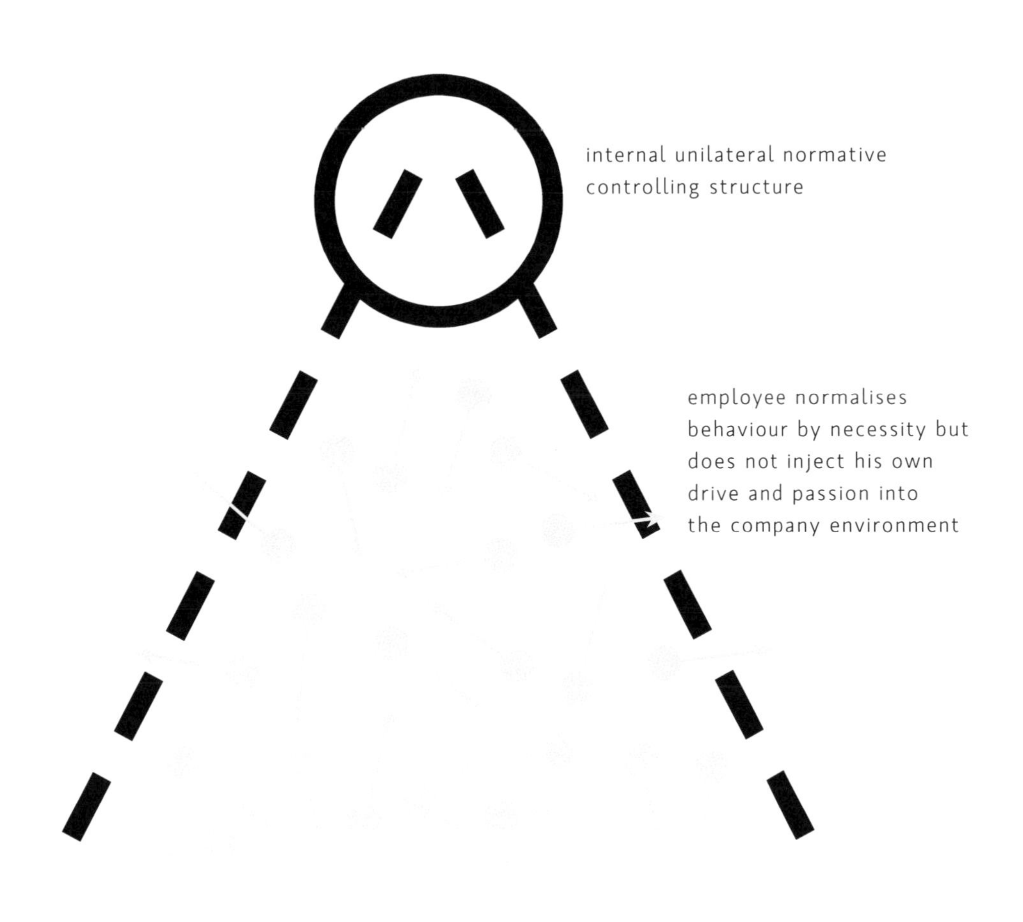

Company coaches: the new spin doctors?

The more friction and irritations exist among a company's employees, the more collective energy is incorrectly or even negatively applied - or perhaps not even applied at all. This results in the company becoming entangled in a web of personal truths and values. Have you looked at your own working environment in this light? What company energy is not threatened by intrigues and lurking power games? Shakespeare's dramas may sometimes appear far-fetched in comparison with what happens on the real life stage where we act out our daily life, but the increasingly successful focus on team building and company coaching justifiably operates within this setting. Company directors are aware that creating a corporate environment now needs to be handled differently and considerable effort is put into the search for new solutions.

In the structure sketched out here, there is an accumulated strength, precisely because communication occurs on two different wavelengths: one from the rational company manager and the other from the experience-oriented employee. You can do your utmost to install structures and communicate values with the aim of attaining a practically organised consensus (see status quo), but you will be unsuccessful in your plan to create a nurturing, dynamic company culture if you do not take into account the emotionally-driven behaviour of each employee.

The individual has, after all, the truth on his side. How can he, in fact, streamline his emotional and experience-based behaviour if he is only addressed from an intellectual framework to adjust this? He will ward off the company structure if he has the feeling of not being understood, supported and nurtured by his employer.

"The individual has, after all, the truth on his side. He will ward off the company structure if he has the feeling of not being understood, supported and nurtured by his employer."

The independent employee

In the current period you can see in the HRM (human resources management) market, just as in society, two reflexes with which the individual reacts towards his environment.

The first group feels secure in their daily routine. These are people who are opposed to every form of intervention by company management and leap into a defensive and resistant reflex. They feel secure within their own set of values and derive a feeling of pleasure and personal value from their own verifiable environment. Any external impulse is experienced as unverifiable and threatening. This group is more likely to be nurtured by a framework which imposes very clear norms which cannot be misunderstood. The culture is implicitly - and sometimes explicitly - dismissive of other convictions as 'this is how it is and no other way'. This kind of group framework thus confirms the individual defensive spatial perception.

On the other hand, it's equally clear that a new generation who, based on the informed choices they make in their life, expresses clear requirements to potential employers. These employees are more aware of their own set of values and permanently expand their world, but drawn entirely from their own conditions and their own framework of convictions. They make it clear what they want and uninterestedly reject those stimuli which do not match their demands. They do not take the trouble to dismiss anything but instead expand their world as much and as fervently as possible with like-minded people, and compatible surroundings and products. They know their list of priorities and organise their life in this way, without compromise. From their sense of self-awareness they often come across as arrogant. "Those new candidates are arrogant, want everything from the start and come with their set of requirements to the first interview," is a frequently heard remark in HRM circles. The potential employee makes the choice here. And the company has to follow: not the other way round, as it used to be.

Of course, two extreme tendencies have been described here. Naturally, there are also a large number of people who display a behaviour which lies between these two reflexes.

Chapter **five** From monitoring to driving

In a word

It all comes down to needing to motivate each employee's efforts in relation to his own evolution and that of the entire work setting. This can be achieved by creating a strong company core, which offers everyone a benchmark to assess and improve his own and his colleagues' performance through his own feelings and experience. Thus, a company heart comes into being which in turn is fortified by each employee's constantly evolving additional value.

The conceptual shift required to resolve the above involves companies learning to create an environment in which every employee feels valued according to his perception, since it is normal for each individual to start from his own emotionally-driven truth. The idea that this leads to excesses where the norm is a total lack of control, is simply an anxiety on the part of senior managers who are obliged to part with their hitherto conventional controls. It is however, the key to exit the chaos in which we wallow when we stick to the current classical control system.

It is self-evident that senior managers play a key role in this situation. It amounts to finding a new language, a new way of organising and communicating so that people whose mindset is subjective and experience-based are able to apply their available energy to the fullest extent in order to enhance the company whilst simultaneously improving themselves. It is exactly this reciprocity which is vital. As a representative, you will need to work purposefully on your company's growth by giving your people the opportunity to develop. It's a fair exchange. It is precisely by supporting people in their individual development that you can access them at the level where they are committed to the group: their own wavelength. Increasingly, people live according to their individual world perspective, so it is necessary that every structure hooks into this and makes a promise to nurture, heighten and strengthen it from the root of its core strength. As a result therefore, the environments constructed will once again win people's trust.

🔊 *"The top floor must raise their game and reach out to the company nerve centre. Its mission is to anchor the company ideology to a transparent and robust core."*

So, how can you install such a new structure. And above all: what does it look like? It amounts to CEOs focusing on the company's modus operandi as their core business. The top floor must raise their game and reach out to the company nerve centre. Its mission is to anchor the company ideology to a transparent and robust core, something to which people can feel allegiance with. This core gives clarity about the common drive and invites every employee to feed into it, whilst also nurturing themselves. It is a benchmark. This enables each individual, through open communication and an experience-focused culture to be supported in the anchor which he adopts for himself as the only correct one: personal observation, personal perception. In this, the company core is not an omniscient, controlling medium, but a nurturing and clear benchmark. It becomes the company heart; a heart where everyone feels he is making a contribution as well as being equally challenged in his own development. Due to the employer, it will also be confronting to suddenly find himself in a structure in which he expressly and personally is addressed in his own evolution. But if the company core reveals that in its essence its aim is gaining strength in unity, then it can at least expect that each employee will do the same.

In this way, 'I' and 'we' remain just as unique as ever, and both parties feel better as a result. Hence, the company becomes a living organism that creates scope and facilitates the role of the employee; subsequently, a win-win situation comes into play. Our result is an improved individual awareness that goes hand in hand with an improved common awareness.

When we give this movement shape, we evolve from a classic top-down structure to an organic centre-peripheral model. The company core encourages everyone to give the best of himself as part of a personal and community development.

Companies willing to prepare for the future need to take two essential steps. Firstly, it amounts to correctly and accurately assigning their core strength. Subsequently, it is important to build a seasoned culture around it. This will lead not only to a mental understanding of the shared awareness but also an emotionally-supported framework is created, resulting in each employee being able to steer their own behaviour with satisfaction.

FROM A TOP-DOWN STRUCTURE TO A CENTRE-PERIPHERAL STRUCTURE

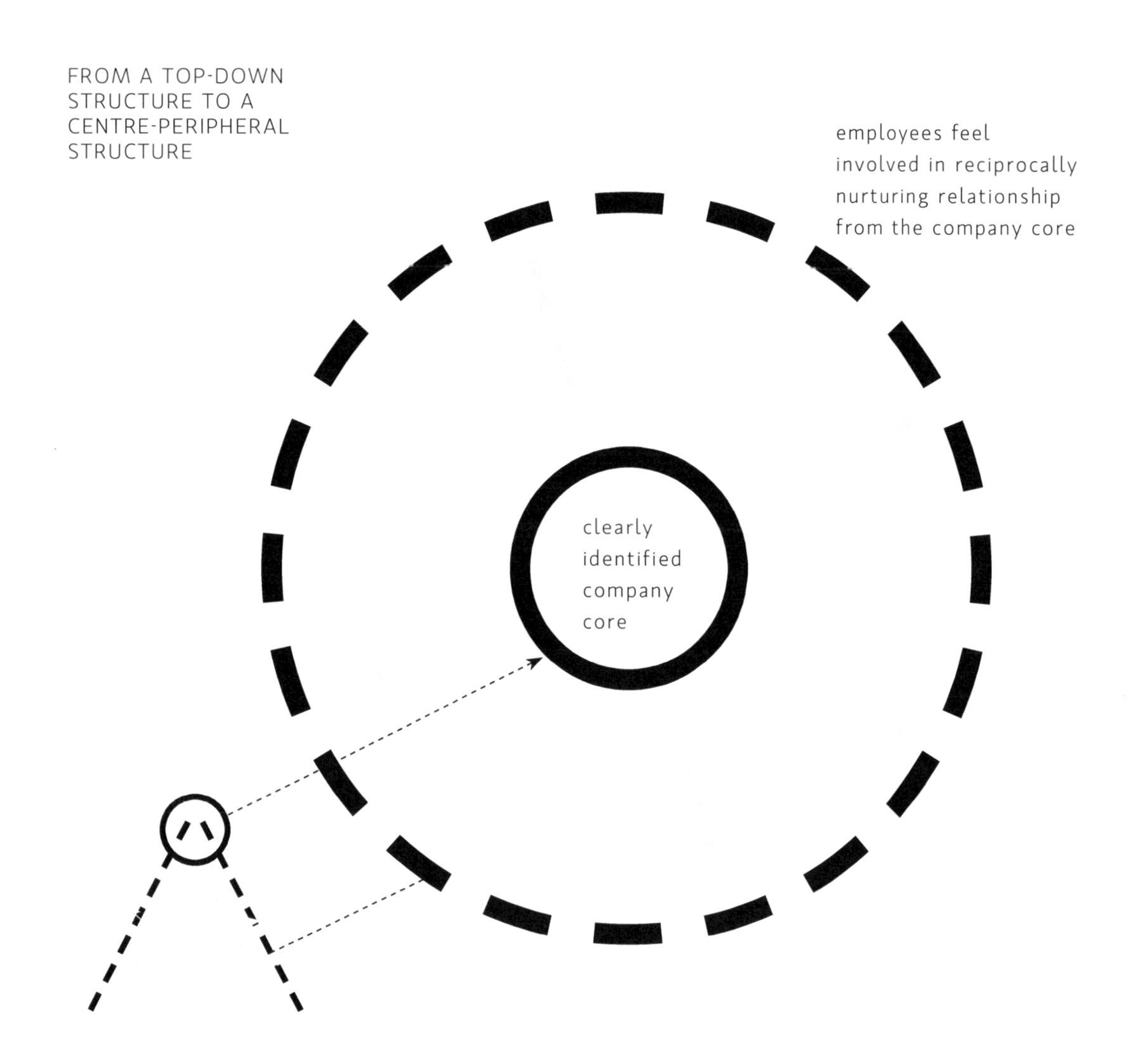

Experiment 3: the fields of potential

We continue to act as an observer of the multi-dimensional sphere from the first experiment. C has now joined A and B. All three are active on the same platform in relation to their relative awareness of it. This develops a new multi-dimensional space. They live on the physically shared platform but based on a completely different world of awareness.

Suppose that we decide to place a tree in the middle of the platform. The tree will have a specific significance in each of their worlds. For A, it's a solid broad pole. In the individual's field of awareness, he is presented with an opportunity to press against the trunk to relieve the pain in his back, which he does. For B, the tree is an interesting research subject. He wonders what is behind the surface and demonstrates this in his behaviour, where he tries to make a hole in the trunk. And for C, the tree holds has no meaning; the individual is completely detached. For him, nothing could be more uninteresting than that brown thing! Each one of them, according to the significance they assign to the tree, finds a number of ways to use it, (or not), to further their own evolution. So we can consider each of their worlds of awareness as a field of potential, which according to their own individual personality and experience will generate the possibilities for specific behaviour in the physical environment.

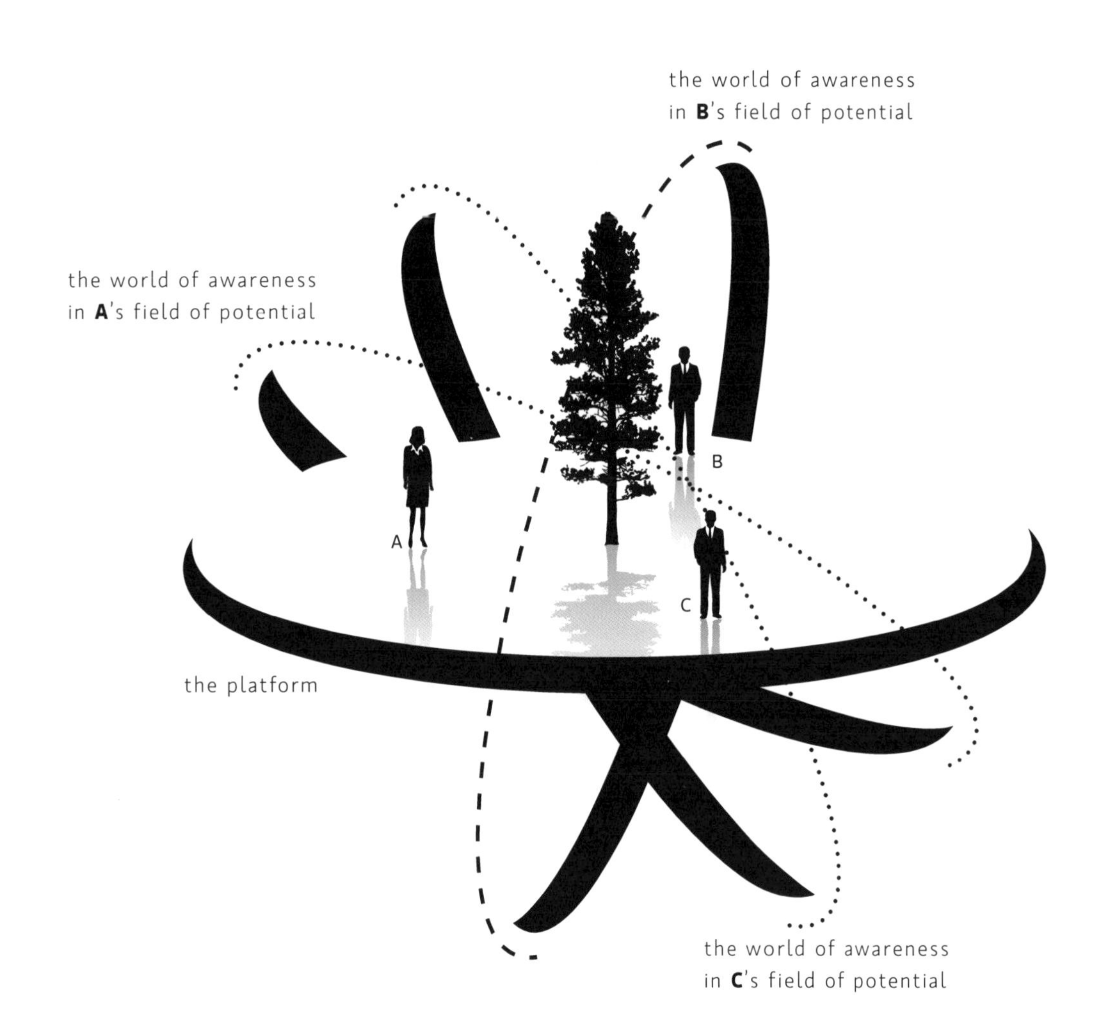
the world of awareness
in **B**'s field of potential
the world of awareness
in **A**'s field of potential
A
B
C
the platform
the world of awareness
in **C**'s field of potential

Suppose that A believes that B is killing the tree by poking about in it, causing him to lose the support for his back. When he tells B this, there is no immediate reason for B to stop. In his world, his actions are relevant and represent his norms and the truth. We note that conflict and tension occur between the truth of the individual's world of awareness and the reality in the shared physical space. To find a solution, they will have to design a way to agree and to evolve.

We can imagine that there is a type of community in the newly formed global space; namely, the sphere. This is the sum of the platform and the world of awareness of each individual who moves on it. We can therefore define this as the common field of potential in the shared physical space. But in the given circumstances of A, B and C it is impossible to create an understanding about this space. As observers, the sphere is visible to us, but not to A, B or C. Each of them lives in his own distinctive world of awareness and the potential that is contained within it. A is therefore unable to perceive the world of awareness of B and C and can neither detect, let alone describe accurately, the sphere environment from this position. The same angle of perception can be applied to the other two. They cannot understand worlds that are unfamiliar or that they do not interact with. There is no clear appreciation about the environment and neither therefore, the objects that are contained therein.

Only through denial and dissociation from one's own awareness can each individual recognise a clear and rationally definable environment. The removal of the individual world of awareness brings the linearly definable space back into existence.

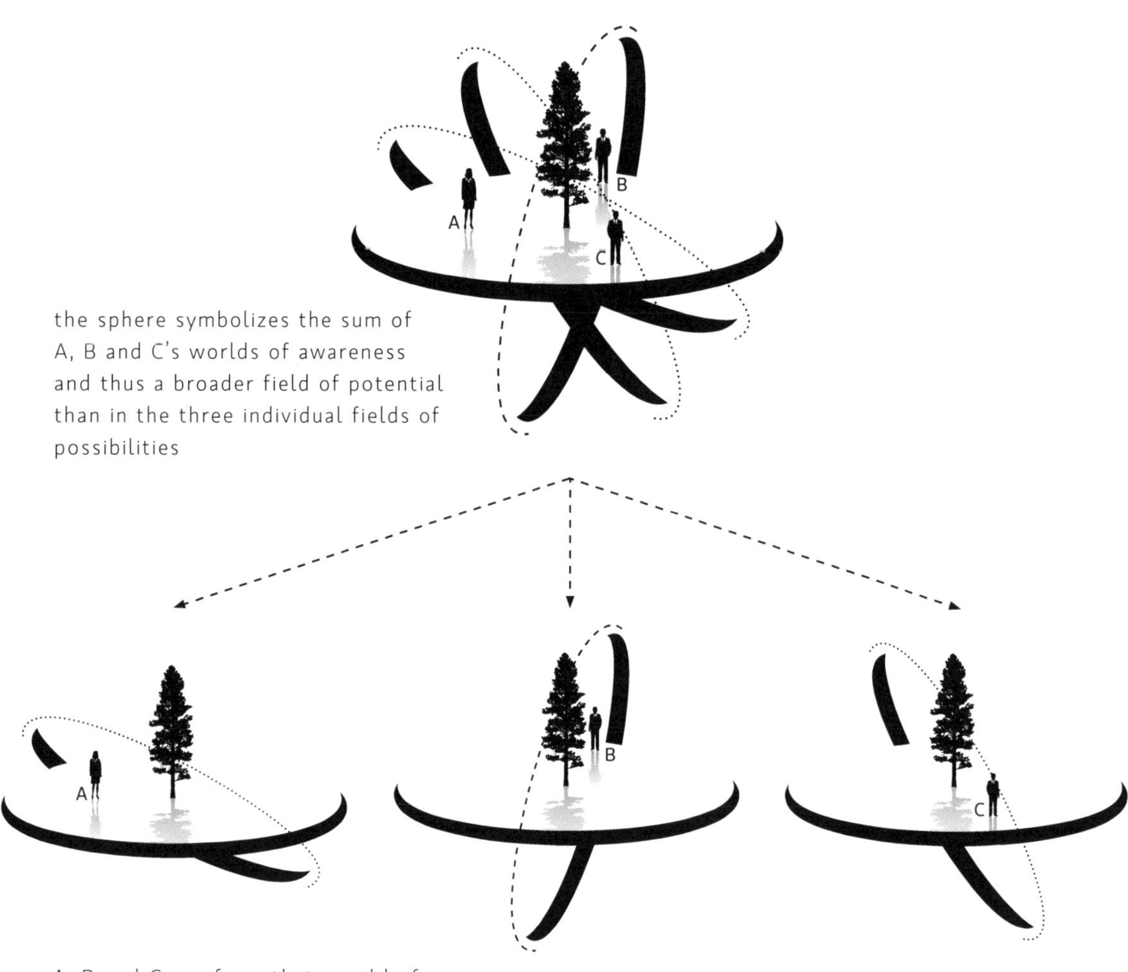

the sphere symbolizes the sum of A, B and C's worlds of awareness and thus a broader field of potential than in the three individual fields of possibilities

A, B and C see from their world of awareness only their own field of possibilities

THE REMOVAL OF THE INDIVIDUAL WORLD
OF AWARENESS BRINGS THE LINEARLY
DEFINABLE SPACE BACK INTO EXISTENCE

The question is how the highly individualistic A, B and C can live together and still address the amassed field of potential encompassed by the sphere. Because A, B and C revolve in their own separate worlds, then the only way forward is to find a degree of commonality.

If we look at the sphere as observers based on this premise, we find a single axis point where the greatest community density is demonstrated, and that point is the centre. Upon analysis, we find that this point is also the core of each separate world of awareness (KA, KB, KC), from the shared platform (KP) and also jointly from these four together (KA + KB + KC + KP). The common core and central point of the sphere, KS, is the combination of the three core fields of potential and the shared physical space. It links the worlds of awareness to the physical and thus symbolises the manifestation of the collective potential.

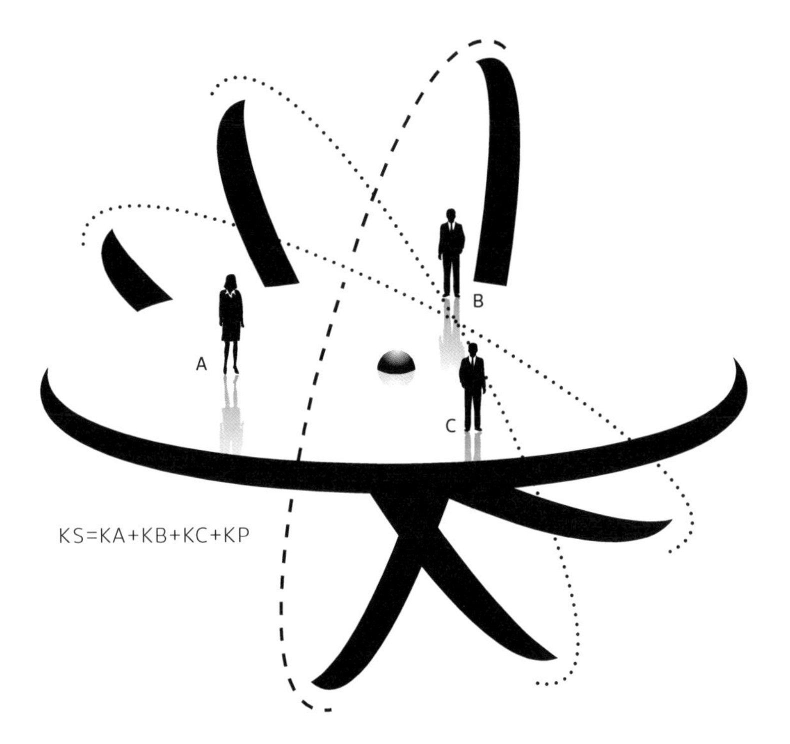

We can say that when A, B and C focus on their own core of awareness this immediately implies recognition from the core of awareness of the other people and the shared physical environment in which the stakeholders operate. This makes perfect sense. 'My world of awareness' can only be assigned in reference to 'your world of awareness'. And one's own individuality can only be assigned by the implication of a 'you' being in the same physical environment. A, B and C exist on the shared platform exclusively in reference to each other. And this is also the case for their worlds of awareness.

From the moment that A, B and C focus on their core they become aware of one another's dynamic. All three individuals can interpret their own behaviour from this awareness by referencing that of the others. This makes it impossible for their perception of the shared physical space to be considered as the only truth. A cannot claim that the truth about this object is that it is undoubtedly a backrest, but instead can state: my truth is that this object, in my view, is a good way to relieve the pain in my back. In other words, they can only express their singularity in the knowledge that this is one version of the truth; namely, theirs. The return to the core implies the awareness of the relativity of the different worlds of awareness. We can even go one step further and say that the relative worlds of awareness in this core point can be regarded as all completely equivalent. Neither A, B nor C can claim that their world of awareness has a greater truth than the others. To do so would, of course, be impossible since there is no absolute form of the truth that can serve as a reference point with which to compare their own perceptions.

One's own field of potential in this core cannot be imposed as the norm, but only as a route to approaching it. As each shares their insights, a common awareness is formed in the core concerning the overall possibilities in which A, B and C are located: the sphere. Indeed, each explains in this core their awareness about their own possibilities as equivalent to that of the others. This concept implies an immediate expansion of one's own awareness. A, B or C cannot say that their understanding of the world remains the same when they are introduced to unknown and clearly equally major truths about the shared physical space. Their view of their reality expands and thus the field of possibilities in their own world of awareness increases. They then learn to understand how each other's behaviour arises from an equivalent individual truth. B realises, for example, that the tree may be used for more than just research, A understands that he does not know what the tree contains and C discovers some new functions for the object which he had hitherto not thought of.

The new opportunities to exploit the common physical space create new experiences in the unique individual worlds of awareness. This creates new personal beliefs and truths that can be equally shared again in the core. This dissemination deepens the common awareness and also enhances the individual's world of awareness. This evolutionary progress can be repeated time and again. It is like a machine in perpetual motion that strengthens individual awareness, resulting each time in a deeper common understanding and vice versa.

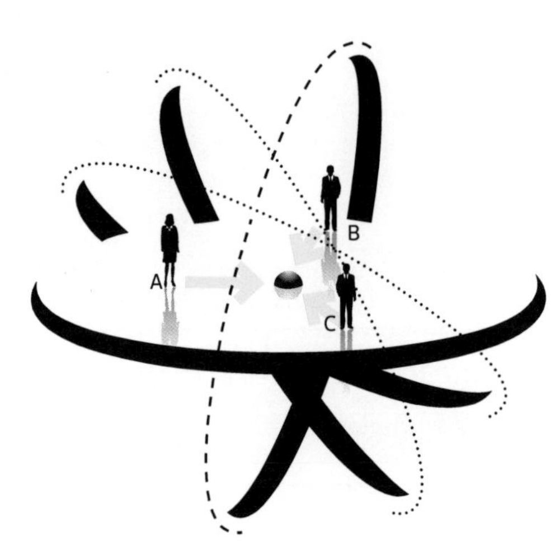

A, B and C turn towards
the common core

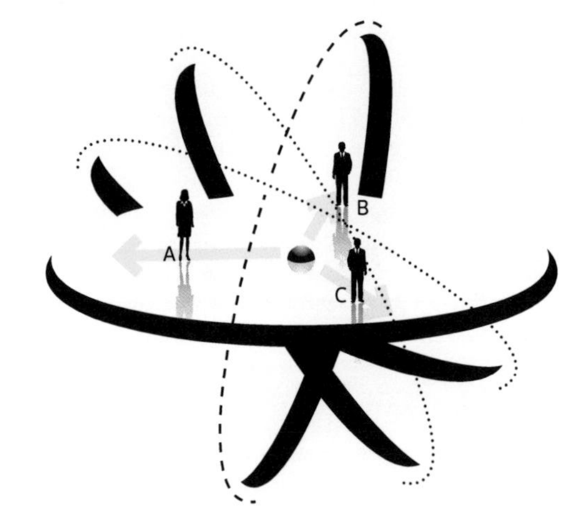

common awareness exists from which
A, B and C are able to compare new
insights with their own experience

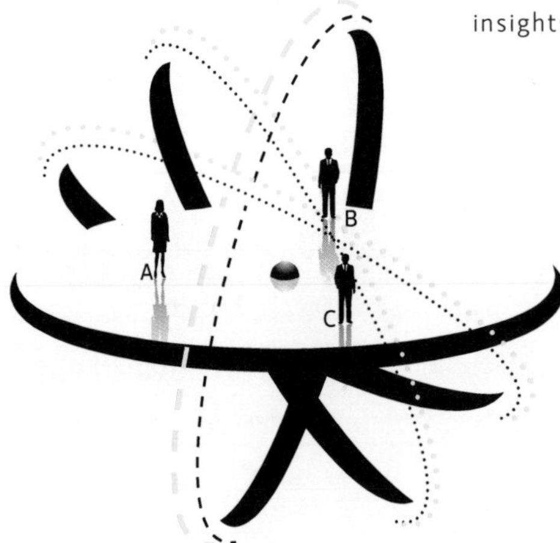

expand personal and communal
awareness fields / fields of potential

Subsequently, a dynamic develops in which individual evolution is inherently tied to common development, without A, B or C feeling obliged to sacrifice their own truth for a common rationalised truth. Each one can proceed utilising their own experience in a shared core of equality to develop their own, and a common awareness. The more the joint core is fuelled, the more focused the energy becomes so that, in the shared physical environment, behaviour can develop that is mutually enriching and yet remains highly individualistic. There is recognition by A, B and C of a constantly expanding world. The sphere is not a linear limited space, but instead is a limitless world of potential for those who are part of it.

This experiment shows that when people share a common space in line with their own individuality, a common relative field of potential is formed that is greater than the shared physical space. This potential is converted into evolutionary energy, when awareness is generated from the individual and common manageable core, into this relative space of potential.

Chapter **six** Assigning the core strength

In a word

The company becomes introspective. In order to create a strong core, it is important to firstly determine the character of the structure. This implies an accurate answer to the questions concerning mission and vision. In addition, the values are determined which serve as a benchmark against which each employee can gauge individual behaviour. In other words, the company values mirror those of each individual.

You cannot of course generate dynamism around a company's heart if you do not know where that organ is, let alone what it represents or how it functions. The key and first step is for the company to look within itself and formulate a clear definition of the mental image of its core strength. In this way, every employee at least knows where to focus their energy and why, and above all, knows what the rewards are. Clearly, it is only from a well-defined framework that a company's own culture can come into fruition.

Je m'exprime donc je crée

Descartes was right when he said that those who think, exist. Anyone who also expresses the thought, takes one step further. That creates a sense of reality. Our first tangible form of creation is to voice an idea or concept, simply because it implies sharing. The idea that is conveyed exists as something between the speaker and the listener. Thus, a polarity is generated which is required for each form of creation. When asked why he is so thoughtful when talking, the American actor John Malkovich said in an interview (free translation): "Never underestimate the power of a word. What I say, exists from the moment I speak out. So I would like to be careful about what I create." The accurate designation of the essence of a business is therefore essential. With it you create a basis for your relationship with each of your employees.

This assignment first of all creates clarity about the identity and substance of the company. These are translated into an accurate articulation of vision, mission and ambition. Answers are given as to 'why do we do this?' and 'where are we going?' Although most companies have already defined a vision, mission and ambition, we have observed that in practice they are often buried deep in everyday operations or that they were operating based upon an incorrect definition of a strategy.

"By assigning its core strength the company creates clarity and tranquillity. There is a reference point created whereby everyone knows exactly what environment he or she works in."

In addition, the key values that determine company behaviour are explicitly laid out. And just as each individual displays awareness, groups also transmit a specific behaviour on the basis of the underlying and often implicit values. By ensuring these values are unequivocally clear, we create a basis for the company culture. The questions of 'how do we do it?' and 'how do we behave?' are answered. This not only filters through on a level of the individual interaction with suppliers and customers, but it also operates at the macro level in relation to market and society.

By expressing these values, the company determines the reference points that each individual can use to assess their behaviour and possibly refine further. These are the anchors which provide for a well-defined understanding of the common culture. It is important that this does not occur with the intention of using this benchmark in a way that impinges on the individuality of the employee. On the contrary, this would offer a basis from which they can identify and develop their own behaviour. It should further facilitate their ability to strengthen and feed into the core item in relation to their commitment and loyalty. In this reciprocity lies the fundamental difference between the unilateral demarcation standard in more classic structures. Conversely, the company identity is in itself boosted by the various individual perceived values. Such a defined framework also provides a reference point for solving potential behavioural conflicts between staff.

The significance of the core

By assigning the business core, we expose the company's DNA. Compare it with any other core centre of a human being, for example. Each of our cells has a specific function and at the same time it contains all the information about who we are, where we come from and what our potential is. It is a fascinating to think that by awakening the DNA-awareness in each cell, it works in a more resilient and collective positive manner. Similarly, in a business, highlighting the understanding of the group-DNA-awareness can ensure that every person who is a part of network is more driven in their own development, which works to reinforce and fortify the group. These DNA studies, analysis and management therefore make for a strong reciprocal action resulting in both individual and group development.

Chapter **seven** Experiencing the core strength

In a word

Being a living organism, the company has to learn to really tap into its employees by addressing them in the language that underpins their behaviour: the language of feelings and experiences. Through an experience-based methodology, each employee will be given the chance, in the first instance, to become aware of his personal behavioural methodology so that he can subsequently share his findings. This nurtures the company, the colleagues and himself with the insights that he thus acquires. Both the individual and the entirety evolve.

Once the core strength is accurately assigned, the business fundamentals are clear. The associated intrinsic values steer both the organisation's and employee's conduct with each other and within their environment. Clearly, it is not sufficient to simply state these values in the hope that a mutual understanding and thus a vibrant business energy will develop. This would lead to each employee translating each value in their own way, injecting their own feelings and experience. Inevitably, only conflict rather than harmony would ensue. Only when we approach people in the business context, recognising and appealing to their implicit personal feelings, will they be able to appreciate how they, and their colleagues are able to satisfy values by adopting specific behaviour. From that moment on, the idea, based on a mutual understanding to work together in a way where each reinforces the other, can take root. A practical and purely theoretical example follows:

Two welders are working in the same company. The explicit business value is craftsmanship. One of the welders translates this as conduct, where he tries to work very quickly and efficiently, despite the occasional errors he makes. These occur simply because he picked up this habit during his training. The second welder exhibits, via an equally relevant personal dynamism, a work ethic wherein he remains very precise, and takes his time to do everything as meticulously as possible. He works slowly, but perfectly. Neither is wrong - neither is incorrect. Each is a craftsman according to his personal perception, and neither thinks about explaining his behaviour in terms of a collection of experiences and beliefs that they carry. Both will have formed opinions about the other's entitlement to be the true craftsman - for one he may seem too quick and to the other, overly precise.

You can guarantee that each will be irritated by the other. They will not collaborate in a way that is fruitful, despite the fact that the employer has clearly marked out the important values. Here is a clear demonstration, where despite the existence of a strong core value, it has failed to be translated into a shared understanding and behaviour.

1. ACTUAL BEHAVIOUR BASED UPON AN EXPLICIT GROUP VALUE

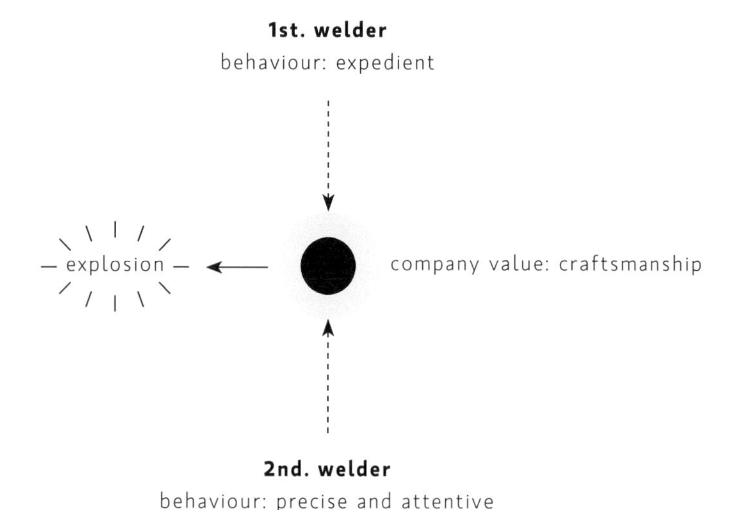

You can try to resolve this by linking each company value to a desired behaviour. In this example, the management could argue that craftsmanship is working efficiently and with care, fulfilling the expectation. This goes some way into clarifying the situation, but it remains incomplete. Just because you have formed rational arguments for trying to create awareness you cannot necessarily expect this to negate an individual's attitude arising often from subconscious feelings. Each type of behaviour is a manifestation of experience driven by subconscious motives. To ensure that employees embrace the core, they should be approached at the level where they control their behaviour: in line with their experience, emotions and their general belief system built up over a period of time. Behaviour is controlled from here, and it is from here that it can also be shaped and changed.

Essentially, we need to delve into the personality dynamics of individuals, if we hope to develop a real awareness about their attitude. This is accomplished by using a very simple but effective methodology of applied experience in which employees have the opportunity to evaluate the set company values versus their own experience. Each person can therefore employ their own sense and interpretation to gauge each value and then immediately articulate which beliefs or experiences they used to translate the value into behaviour. This gives rise to a new awareness. They realise that they have translated a certain value in their specific and unique way and that this has grown out of an acquired knowledge and experiences from the past. What was previously implicit behaviour is now conscious behaviour. The awareness about their own unconscious motivations is the first and most vital step.

A second step concerns the sharing of these individual insights. In this example, the welders are invited to speak about their perception of craftsmanship. In the beginning, they express which behaviour they exhibit and why they acted in this way.

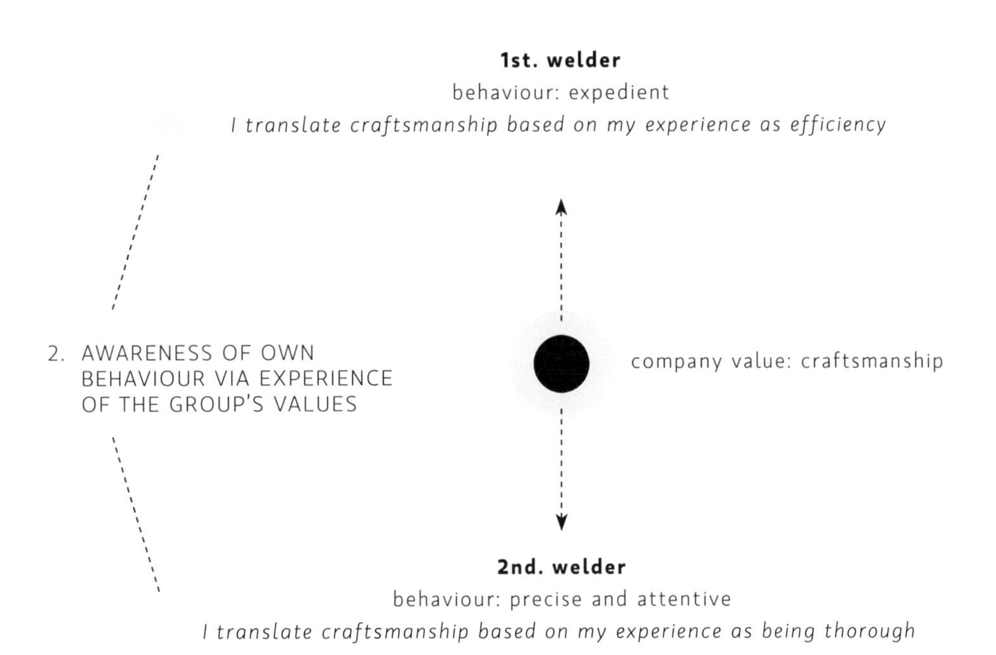

This creates both a more pronounced self-awareness and a greater understanding of each other's composition. It makes for a type of reciprocity where each person can facilitate the evolution and stimuli for their behaviour via an appreciation of the other's. One's own truth is enriched by this new experience. Moreover, the central company value will be nurtured in its meaning through the insights of the employees. In this example for instance, it is clear that a more balanced and more lively notion of the company value 'craftsmanship' is formed.

The company kindles a broader personal and communal awareness through a solid experienced-based methodology. Here, we can immediately see the added value that a strong business core can impart to each employee. In their daily work, both welders are as committed as they were previously, in their own unique way. Now that they understand how they can each influence one another via a common framework, they will attune their behaviour to each other so that they are complimentary; ever more aware of their attitude, they adopt a number of strengths from their colleague. The efficient welder will increase his satisfaction by making something well in addition to producing something quickly. The precise welder finds it a desirable challenge to produce something quickly in addition to producing it well. And if one of them fails in this personal challenge, the other one is ready to step in and assist by lending his talents. Above all, it is now possible for them to communicate with each other. These dynamics will repeat time and time again and enable the welders to permanently amplify their own and each other's consciousness of the different company values.

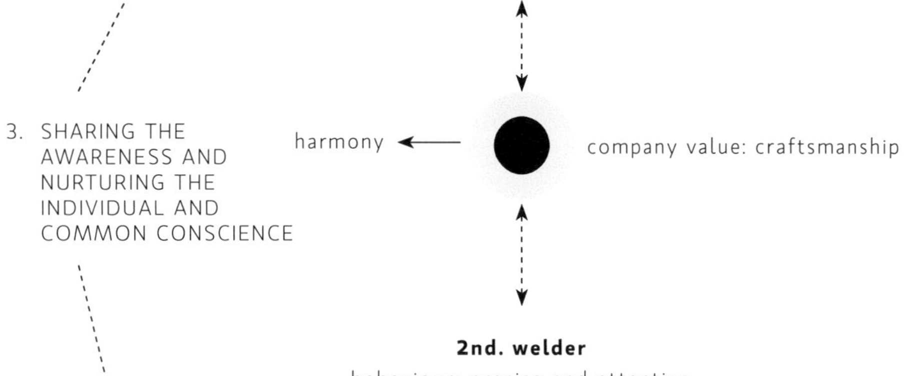
1st. welder
behaviour: expedient
I translate craftsmanship based on my experience as efficiency
I bring efficiency to the core and am open to thoroughness
3. SHARING THE AWARENESS AND NURTURING THE INDIVIDUAL AND COMMON CONSCIENCE
harmony
company value: craftsmanship
2nd. welder
behaviour: precise and attentive
I translate craftsmanship based on my experience as being thorough
I bring a high level of precision to the core and am open to efficiency

Ultimately, the core that becomes a beating heart radiates clarity, nourishing everyone; and it is at the same time supported by everyone. The chief objective of working for the success of the boss has no currency, instead the focus is the success of each individual and the group as a whole, both financially and emotionally on a rational and emotional level. The group's creative energy acts upon and extracts the individual awareness and understanding on a continual basis, honing and enriching it. The result is an ongoing personal and collective evolution. Feelings of happiness and success are cultivated here because of the opportunity to stimulate and grow individual and joint potential.

🔈 *"When this is done properly, the process will facilitate companies and businesses to profile themselves for what they are: strong, visible, dynamic and successful brands."*

Part 3

the ceo-model

or the energetics of human group behaviour unravelled

Chapter **eight** The creative energy organisation model

In a word

All human behaviour is based in a broader context on eight identical universal values. These values form a ratio with each other in a specific dynamic depicted in the ceo-model. In terms of behaviour, they create the energy that can either lead to conflict or harmony. In this, every employee acts as the energy conductor for the value. An awareness of the manner in which everyone converts a value into a particular behaviour makes it possible to direct and share the energy. This allows a movement towards structures where each individual's energy is effortlessly applied to the development of personal and communal strength.

Thus, each company assigns its core energy and builds a seasoned culture around it. Determining the values is crucial in this. We assume that there has to be an identical value reference, which serves as a benchmark for driving the group energy and individual behaviour. This reciprocity is inherent in this new evolution where there is no longer a separation between a person's dynamic and that of his environment. Both integrate the relationship and the sense of arriving at a code of behaviour that sustains the individual and the other team members. Based on the same values, we achieve an evolution in the awareness of the individual and the group in which they function.

"My individual world and the one in which I live and work is one and the same and functions in the same way. This reciprocity is inherent in the new evolution, where there is no longer a separation between a person's dynamic and their environment."

This immediately necessitates a universal set of values, which surpasses, in its essence, the specificity of each clearly defined environment and of each individual. It goes without saying that a board of directors who have the interests of the entire organisation at heart, will not randomly determine which and how many values should be applied. It would once more be an illustration of the classic one-way street in which a company's senior management imposes a certain framework, which should also be used for personal evolution. Conversely, it is equally illogical that the employees, through their own interests, would impose their value priorities based on their own intuition onto the group. Furthermore, the individual is unable to impose his own feelings onto the organisation. Thus, it would be harmful for one of the two to determine the criteria on which he and the other evolves. This generates precisely that duality which we now wish to shed. We are now seeking a central benchmark, which may not and cannot be claimed by the players who have to work with it.

It seems plausible therefore that a value dynamic can be universally applied in every environment and to every person. It's a kind of stock set of values which can be moulded to fit a certain environment, but are essentially the same. After thorough conceptual and empirical research, we have settled upon a universal benchmark. It involves a matrix of eight determinant values, which forms the cornerstone for every reciprocal fruitful collaboration, in every type of environment. Any behaviour of an individual or group finds its origins in the perception of one of these defining values. They form the basis for communal and individual development, for the evolution of the highest personal and communal consciousness.

The creative energy organisation model, the ceo-model in short, not only assigns these eight values but also reveals their key underlying dynamic, from which the group's creative energy can be awakened. Evidently, in analyzing this, a sophisticated play of reciprocal energy transfer unfolds, where personal and communal awareness go hand in glove with an increasingly powerful and effortless evolution. Clearly, here is a model in which each value has its place and secures a clear relationship with the other values. In this sense, we can consider it as a real formula for arriving at a behaviour mix, which helps develop the individual and communal strength in each environment. This is the motor that drives creative energy.

BASIC CEO-MODEL

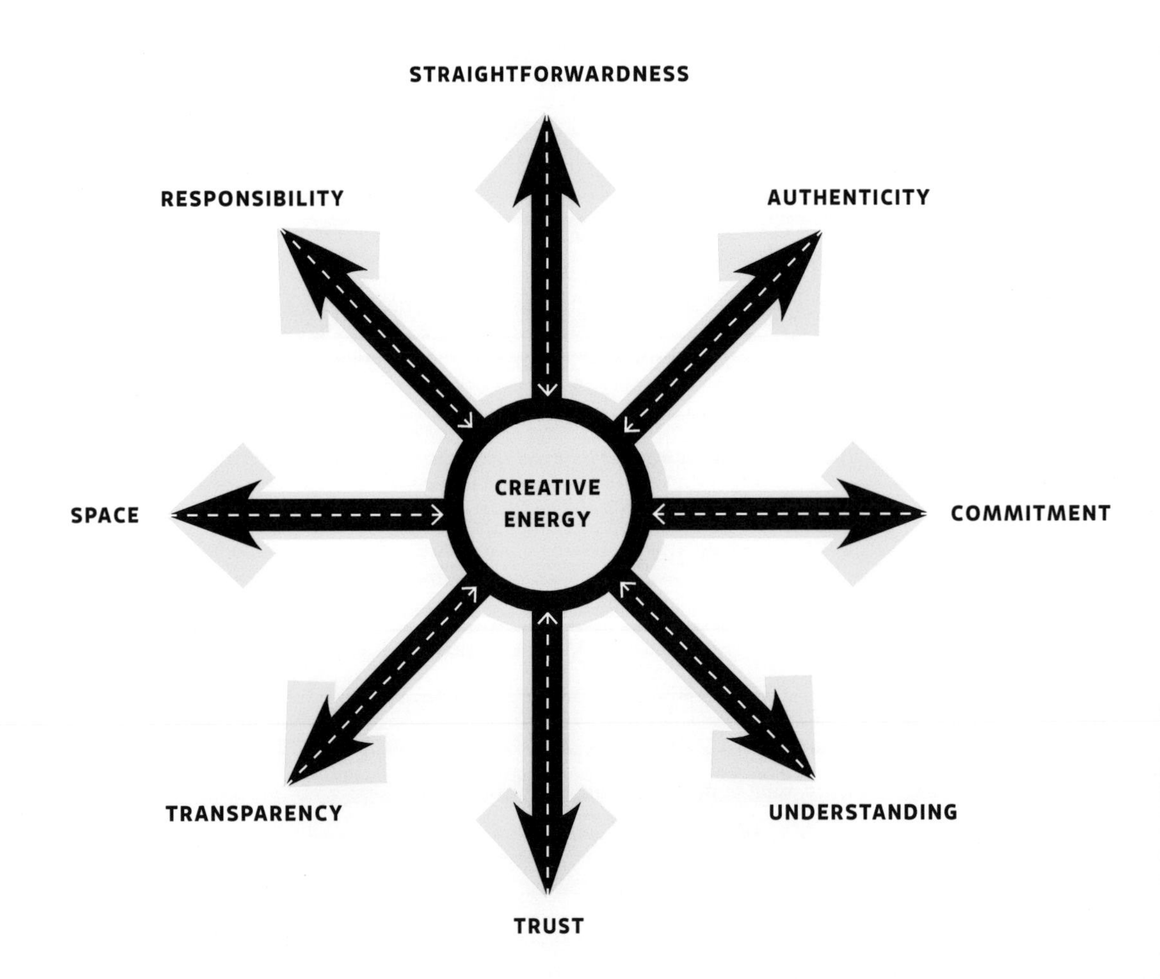

The motor of creative energy

It is obvious that this model is not sufficient to provide a blueprint for the company culture when you wish to stimulate creative energy. It is the engine that must be started and driven. No energy can be generated simply by installing a structure. It is triggered by employee behaviour based on the experience that the employee subconsciously links to each of these values. These are, as it were, the energy conductors. The fusing of different individual behaviours can lead to conflicts, which result in a loss of energy. But equally, they can lead to nurturing and fusion. To achieve this, the methodology already described to engender the experience is applied and is linked to the eight determinant values. They are like benchmarks that can confer any conduct with conscious roots. The ceo-model visualizes this dynamic.

Firstly, each employee is given the opportunity to become aware of the behaviour they link to each value. Clearly, when behaviour is generated subconsciously from a value, its direction cannot be predetermined. However, when one is aware of this process, the behaviour, and thus the energy linked to it can be aimed intelligently and effectively.

Through perception-based guidance everyone is given an opportunity to consider how they experience each value. Each person can then verify for themselves which of the eight values they show a natural preference for. In this way, they acquire an insight into the mental and emotional blockages which impede the complete development of their strength. Examining this broader view, they are in a position to share their own dynamic with the working environment. In other words, this forms an awareness about personal dynamic. They can begin to think along the lines of: 'Oh, so this is the way I convert that value into behaviour'. Because it involves the eight basic values from which each person's behaviour develops; the individual is given every opportunity to get a complete overview of their own behaviour and development dynamic.

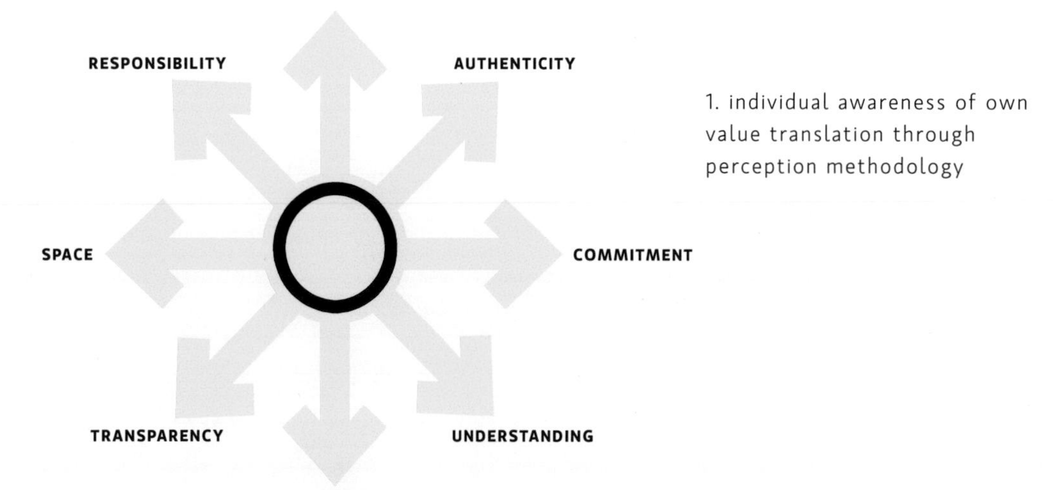

1. individual awareness of own value translation through perception methodology

The next step is the creation of an environment in which the individual's awareness is shared with the other members of the group. We illustrate this activity in the model by the arrows pointing inwards. This creates a mutual understanding and an insight into how people behave, so that the person begins to think along the lines of 'Oh, so this is the way my colleagues convert that value into behaviour'. In the centre of the diagram, we show the space where all personal insights come together. Thereby, a common awareness is formed wherein all individual experiences can be evaluated.

BASIC CEO-
MODEL

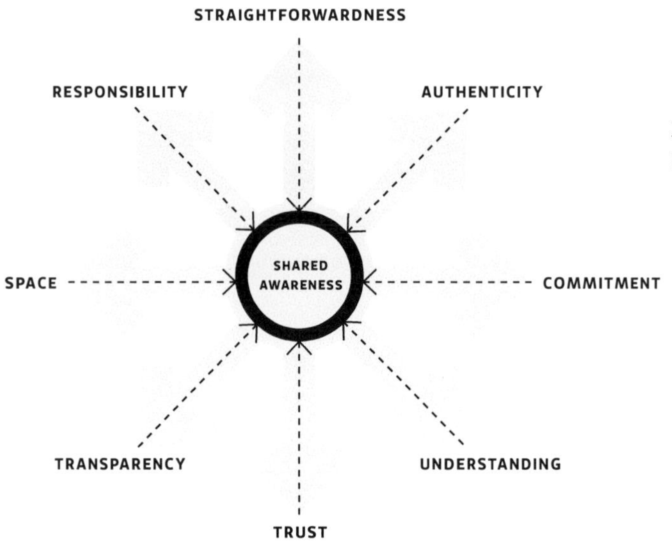

2. parts of individual awareness
linked creation shared awareness

Like this, each individual finds their own interpretation of the value that is deeper and more complete than the one he or she held previously and believed to be correct. Due to this, their own behaviour is nurtured and deepened, to provide the energy to once again strengthen the communal core. This growing common understanding translates into a strong and purposeful appearance of the group through which every behaviour enables total loyalty not only to them, but also to the organisation. The expansion of individual awareness and the increasingly powerful appearance of the common core, are depicted through arrows pointing outward.

CEO-MODEL
DYNAMIC

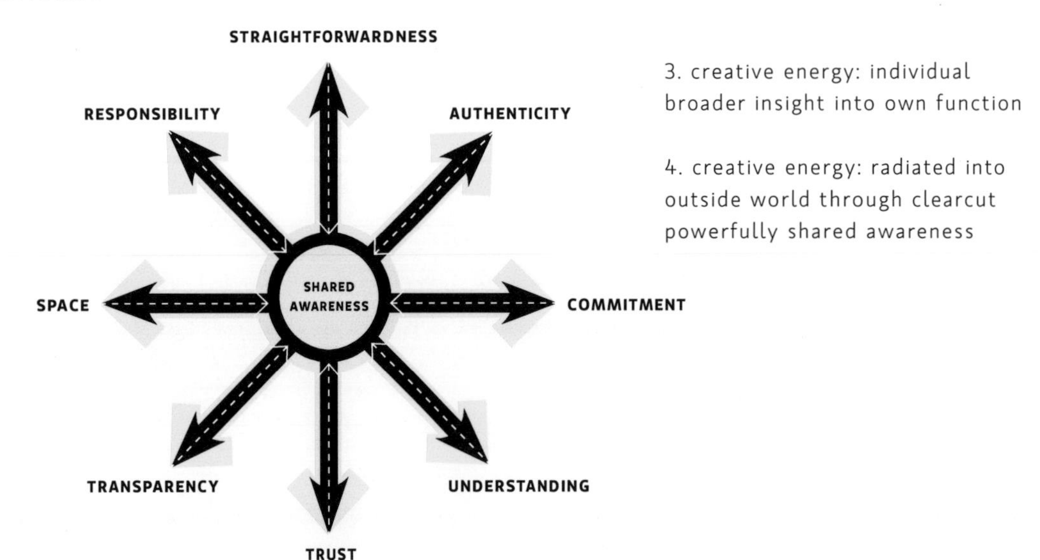

With thanks to Pythagoras

It was he who gave mankind the insight, by devising models, to clarify and explain concepts. Among many other talents, this brilliant philosopher already attempted in the 6th century BC to distil his idealism using diagrammatic language. He was convinced that the laws responsible for creating order and chaos were as good as intangible and incomprehensible to man. He considered it his mission to decipher this and to translate it as clearly as possible into concepts, representations and abstract ideas that people could understand. Clearly, it would be a gross understatement to say that with this work he made it possible for philosophy and science to continue for roughly two thousand years. His theorems and findings have indeed been accepted for centuries as unshakeable truths and profound philosophical insights. It's fascinating to think that this man was already thinking along the lines of working across the disciplines, so very long ago.

This ensures the ceo-model is visualized as a creative energy machine that is in perpetual motion, working to produce a deeper personal and communal awareness. The method makes for a dynamic driving process that encompasses the idea of an ongoing burgeoning of personal and communal strength. In light of this, it is probably more correct to call it an evolutionary model. Each organisation is a living organism, where a changing constellation of individuals creates a balance, facilitating individual steps taken together. As the conduct unfolds, everyone can inject personal energy into the company environment. A distinction no longer exists between the subconsciously emotionally driven individual world and the consciously rationally driven company environment. They are fused together. One can no longer speak of an energy devouring dynamic in which the personal world has to be protected from the environment through hidden agendas and machinations. The result is that everyone can apply their energy in a straightforward way in the unified world in which they live.

The ceo-model conceptualises the unified DNA of the human individual and group awareness. It provides a means of indicating and stimulating our evolution in the coming era.

After universal rights, man's universal values

We are concerned here with a new universal value framework that enables people and communities to live and work successfully and happily together. Prosperity is generated because a great deal more personal energy is available and fruitfully applied to attain goals. And the prosperity is furthered because everyone feels that their personal potential is validated and can be cultivated on a permanent basis.

After universal rights, perhaps now is the time to apply man's universal values. In this, the social organs of government are aimed at the cultivation of creative energy through the installation and operation of the polar forces circumscribing these values. This will involve some mental gymnastics, if this truly demonstrates that in decades to come, human evolution will receive the means to function on different levels of awareness from those we are currently work with. Society and the individual are addressed in an authentic, seamless and challenging experience of success and happiness.

"The creative energy organisation model (ceo-model) shows a universal criterion for prosperous and successful living and working together. The key extended by this model provides access to energy, which enables people to optimally project their ideas and projects onto the world, irrespective of whether it is an organisation, a company or a community."

Chapter **nine** Four polar forces analyzed

In a word

A company can make the ceo's values personal by interpreting them without losing their essential significance. The positioning of the values in the model cannot be changed. In fact, the behaviour coming from one value holds a polar relationship with the opposite value. Thus, four polar forces develop, each responsible for the creation of a particular aspect of the group awareness.

The organisation's core managers have an exceptionally important role to play in installing and maintaining the ceo-dynamic. Indeed, they are the representatives and guardians of the group awareness. It's their task to form a more profound understanding of the system provided, to install this model as the engine for individual and communal evolution. Indeed, there can be no growth in communal awareness if its parameters are not clearly assigned. Only in this way can a core come into being where all individual perceptions are amassed and directed.

Bearing these facts in mind, it is important that the company does not indiscriminately adopt the universal values to assign its cultural core. It is far better to consider them as value clusters, which must have a specific interpretation suited to the company's uniqueness, but in which the essence of the basic value can be identified. It is in the correct and nuanced development of the significance of each basic value, that each company can make the model its own.

Nevertheless, it is important to respect the specific area, which each value occupies in the ceo-model. For example, you cannot replace commitment with responsibility. Undoubtedly, it is true that each behavioural value can be potentially repelling or nurturing when matched with the anti-pole shown in the model. This means that behaviour based on a single value has the potential to strengthen or weaken the behaviour developed from a polar value. The four polar expansion forces are each responsible for the creation and evolution of a specific aspect of the group awareness and for the generation of part of the creative energy. This polar character is an essential quality of the ceo-model. It is a law of physics that we are borrowing from here to human awareness. In the ceo-model, the arrows pointing inwards can be considered as the representation of the polar dynamic between diametrically opposed values.

"It is the law of polarisation in physics, considered determinant in the creation of energy, that we apply, as it were, to human awareness."

BASIC CEO-MODEL

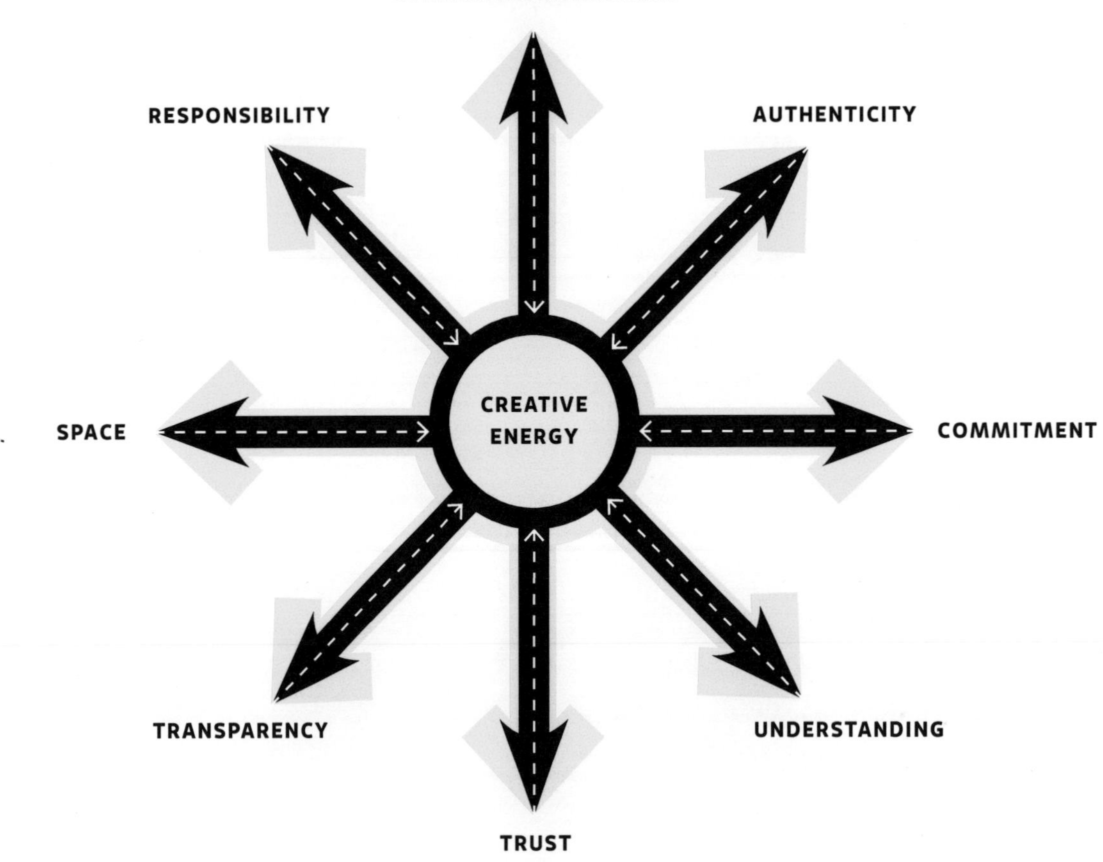

FOUR POLAR EXPANSION FORCES

STRAIGHTFORWARDNESS
behaviour which stems from straightforwardness has a polar relationship with behaviour which is a translation of the value trust
TRUST
behaviour which stems from trust has a polar relationship with behaviour which is a translation of the value straightforwardness

AUTHENTICITY
behaviour which stems from authenticity has a polar relationship with behaviour which is a translation of the value transparency
TRANSPARENCY
behaviour which stems from transparency has a polar relationship with behaviour which is a translation of the value authenticity

COMMITMENT
behaviour which stems from commitment has a polar relationship with behaviour which is a translation of the value space
SPACE
behaviour which stems from space has a polar relationship with behaviour which is a translation of the value commitment

RESPONSIBILITY
behaviour which stems from responsibility has a polar relationship with behaviour which is a translation of the value understanding
UNDERSTANDING
behaviour which stems from understanding has a polar relationship with behaviour which is a translation of the value responsibility

In order to consolidate this and all the other aspects of the ceo-model theory, we analyze the polar forces by looking at the determinant aspects of each value in detail.

The basic significance: Here we give the definition of each value. It relates to the inherent character, which must be retained in any interpretation.

Translation in subconscious behaviour: How do we convert this value in our daily subconscious behaviour? We give a number of examples of possible breakdowns in communication when each individual behaves based purely on his own truth and converts the value concerned into subconscious behaviour which cannot be guided. In addition, the often limited or malformed perception of significance of a certain value in the traditional company environment is indicated.

Shared perception of the value: What happens if we become aware of the individual behaviour linked to this value? We describe the effect of the sketched perception methodology on the individual and the group. For each value, clarification will be given for each part of the shared awareness. From this, each employee can improve his own awareness and behaviour. The group will also be able to behave in a more clear-cut manner at the building of its relationship both with the market and society.

Polar force dynamic: How does polarity influence this process? The relationship with and the importance of the polar value will be clarified.

Role of the core: What role does the company core play in this? We map out the recurring task of the company core to act as creator and driver of creative energy.

Straightforwardness vs. trust

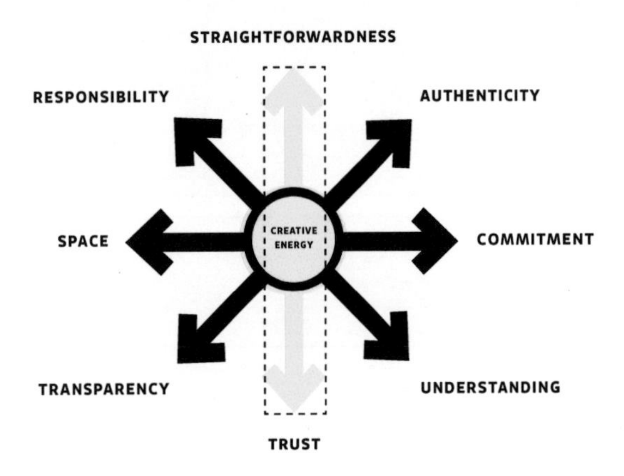

Straightforwardness

Description

This value makes us immediately think of the symbol for our emotion: the heart. We consider this to be the place where our passion lies, it embodies the fire that every person has within them to develop their talents. It is the basis of the emotions that our subconscious emits. To 'open' this up to the outside world is not that simple. It constitutes a very vulnerable part of our personality and we therefore do everything to steadfastly protect it. The challenge to be straightforward is fuelled by the fear that everyone possesses, of having their heart trampled on.

Translation in subconscious behaviour

Real openness involves expressing one's feelings and this is not obvious in the rationalised view of the society in which we have grown. This is vividly apparent in the economic world where it is indeed rare to witness genuine expression of feeling within a company. Attempting to display such emotion is perceived as inappropriate, weak and unprofessional, simply because in a rationally structured environment there is little room for it. That domain belongs to one's private life.

We have learned to express our feelings in the workplace in as rational a manner as possible or to suppress them. We try to think them through in the hope that they'll disappear, but they continue to persist. Often, they lodge as an increasing bundle of pent-up or unexpressed energy, which sooner or later needs to be vented. Expression exhibits differently in each individual and at different rates. Thus, there are people who ventilate their feelings through often chaotic and unrestrained emotions. Consider the short-tempered manager or the whining secretary. Or the reverse. Others simply change the context, if they do not find a vehicle for their expression. There are also many people who suffer physically due to pent-up feelings. No physician today can deny that psychosomatic disorders lie at the root of absenteeism and sickness. These are just some of the ways people respond to the enforced suppression of our feelings.

Much of the time, personal energy is used to suppress one's own feelings, rather than expressing it in an intelligent way. The latter would be supported by the group and be to everyone's benefit. You often find that anyone who makes personal admissions of feeling is often ostracised from the group culture and is considered less suitable for the job. By speaking out, one's position is compromised.

Shared experience

Suppose you end up in an environment where space is given to measure one's own mood and to express this individualistically. Then the personal energy that would otherwise remain without an outlet for expression, suddenly finds a proper place. It is considered as an integral part of the group energy. Due to the inclination to examine one's own emotions and to share these with others, each individual creates a broader understanding of his own position and also that of his colleagues.

If everyone in the specific environment follows this pattern, a shared awareness develops regarding the significance and perception of this value. This creates a clear, shared emotional identity. From this world of collective emotions, everyone extracts the insights he needs to frame and improve the personal perception. My drive and my feelings are fuelled by understanding: 'our drive' and 'our feeling'. Personal energy is not used for defence or disguise but to contribute precisely to the whole and to make progress oneself. Due to the fact that their own core sense is validated in the group process, each employee can engage his own passion, so that his stake and involvement versus the whole will be many times more intense. The more straightforward one is, the greater the mutual trust grows. The energy is released.

Organisations with a strong straightforward culture will be able to allow themselves to be open and express their vulnerability to the outside world. Their frequency of communicating also addresses and connects with the clients', and potential clients', feelings.

Polar force dynamic: trust

The person who exhibits straightforwardness wears his heart on his sleeve and is vulnerable. Naturally, it is not a quality that is readily exhibited. To do this, you need to have confidence in your environment. The person without that confidence cannot possibly enter into this mindset. The fear of being able to 'lay bare' the very essence of one's own feelings, is too great. The protective guard is quickly imposed. Alternatively, anyone unable to be straightforward does not reveal the essence of his feelings and, as a result, cannot expect to feel trusted in his environment.

Trust

Description

Trust is often considered as an 'unspoken reality'. Either it's there or it isn't. This value is based on having faith in the people around you: you believe in them and in their good intentions, you trust that they do not harbour negative thoughts. This also involves self-belief or self-confidence.

Translation in subconscious behaviour

Every person joining a group carries around his own behaviour, which translates from the individual personality dynamic into a large or small amount of trust both inwardly and towards the group. In every working environment you will spot 'the gullible colleague' who will believe everything they hear, the more unattainable co-worker who you find rather untrustworthy or the one that loses his self-confidence at the slightest mistake.

Typically, in a professional environment, it is not usual to invest anyone with too much trust, nor to place your trust too quickly. The person who starts off with a healthy dose of mistrust, protects himself in advance. There is then no need to blame himself when things go wrong. However, the person who does not have a sense of gaining complete confidence will equally display their own confidence more reticently.

The person with extreme self-confidence will make their presence strongly felt in the group and will not be completely popular. His co-workers will magnify the slightest mistake made by 'the man that does it all' and thus place little trust in him. Consequently, the concerned man will go the extra mile and have to make an additional effort to try and prove himself. For those with poor self-esteem the excessive self-confidence of this colleague will compensate for their own lack of it. It will give them the opportunity to hover in the background and keep a low profile.

These are but a few examples of how we experience this value. When we start out using only our own belief system to streamline our behaviour, we will always cocoon ourselves in the cosy status quo of our familiar habits. There can be no hint of any evolution in our personal, let alone communal behaviour. We are thrown into a context where we can decide whether to give of ourselves to a greater or lesser degree, depending on our own individually built-up behaviour dynamic. Any individual energy is exhausted to consolidate the individual experience of the particular value in an environment which is considered not entirely safe. It is a vicious circle of a recurring interpersonal dynamic. We find ourselves in a stalemate in which the defences of our self-righteousness grow larger and stronger.

Shared experience

You develop awareness about yourself when you are offered the opportunity to understand how you give and receive trust and to assess your levels of self-confidence. An environment that fosters this and also helps to ensure that employees share that understanding, develops a powerful new joint consciousness. When we are able to trust from this perspective, the self-awareness of each individual is nurtured. In the same setting, everyone can perform his task with a healthy dose of self-confidence. The person with little faith in himself will receive the trust that is necessary to build on his self-esteem. The one who comes to realise that it is wiser to temper his large ego, will notice that he automatically gains more trust from his colleagues.

A clear significance and perception of this value develops, enhanced by everyone: 'My trust' becomes 'our trust'. Belief in one another ratifies each individual. We discover both our own and our colleagues' dynamism and from thereon in, we can enrich our own demeanour. Nobody is obliged to play tough, due to the propagation of strong mutual trust.

Companies that have a strong culture of mutual trust are able to present themselves not as a naïve organisation, but always as confident and reliable partners for the market it is engaged in and most especially for society in general.

Polar force dynamic: straightforwardness

What you need in order to create trust is straightforwardness. A person who is comfortable about exposing their feelings, passion, vulnerability and can reveal their more intimate characteristics is a trustworthy person. But you cannot expect that self same person to be open and straightforward if they receive mistrust in return.

The role of the core

But there is always a bit of a catch! When you embark on a relationship based upon the polar force, it is tricky to be the first to enter into the exposing dynamic. The quandary is: *if you are straightforward, I will trust you, but how do I know I can trust you if you don't trust me …* - it's like the story of the chicken and the egg! Business can play a crucial role, here. It is the company's duty to integrate the correct flexibility within the value balance between straightforwardness and trust in building the corporate identity, and vice versa, to be consistent in creating a truly 'living' culture around it.

When this is done it creates a culture where it is not necessary for one employee to wait for the other to extend trust or demonstrate straightforwardness. The business simply expects that experiencing these values strengthens and endorses the core. In exchange, the company core guarantees each individual the security that this culture of give and take will not be abused. The new standard does not in any case require enforcement of rational rules but does invoke the appropriation of a specific self-examination and empowering of the group dynamic.

This results in a portion of the creative energy in the core that generates a common reality, enhancing clarity for the individual's and group's feelings and trust. The energy normally used to create barriers is now functional and nourishing, boosting the whole company and the development of every employee. It is clear that organisations whose members work together based upon a platform of resolute trust, faith and straightforwardness, develop a stronger and unambiguous common unity that is of benefit to everyone.

By developing such strength these groups are, in turn, able to engage with the outside world in a trusting and straightforward relationship. Based on appropriate self-confidence they are able to act with an open, assertive and impassioned style with the customer, the market and society.

Authenticity vs. transparency

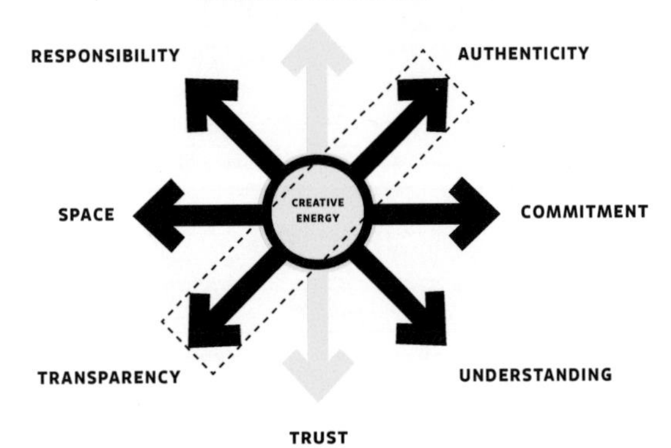

Authenticity

Description

Autheniticity is most commonly defined as simply 'being who you are'. Someone who is authentic is aware of their uniqueness and believes they have the right to exist in the environment in which they function. They sketch out an identity for themselves from the acceptance that they have a specific personal dynamic, values and truths.

Translation in subconscious behaviour

The perception of originality depends greatly on the environment in which we operate. It goes without saying that you might feel much more at home in one place than in another. The more insecure we feel in a certain environment, the less inclined we are to reveal our authenticity. Thus, we easily find ourselves in situations where we believe we can better act out our right of existence when we do not appear completely as we truly are. Company environments offer excellent examples of where we only reveal those aspects of ourselves which amplify the image our colleagues receive from us. But this is precisely what creates a labyrinth of unfathomable personalities where no-one really retains their authenticity.

Furthermore, experience has taught us when to claim our authenticity in our own way. Some people feel compelled to emphasize their uniqueness, by dressing conspicuously or behaving in a way, which is consistently at odds with that of the group. Compare this with an adolescent who realises that they are 'someone'. Often, those who shout the loudest in a group are those with the least sense of a right of existence. Sometimes they also have an extreme form of identity awareness. In both cases, they each need to convince themselves and their environment that there is no-one like them. That they are one of a kind. They use their energy to prove this repeatedly, through an extreme and confrontational expression of their own identity. The environment refuses to accept this person's perception of themselves and conflicts occur. This results in them trying even harder to show their identity, which is conveyed in their behaviour based on their own personal dynamic. Thus, we end up in a vicious circle of confrontation.

What can also occur is that a layer of that self-image is translated in an impulse to seek out similarities in every context they are involved in, so that their attitude levels out to match that of the group. Here, the right of existence is linked to the need to be accepted. They become part of the whole. The energy is used to adapt personal identity to the setting. The alert person will be quick to pick up on this, which will result in an ongoing acceptance and increasingly strong identification with the group and this will constantly deny their individuality.

Neither of these two expressions of originality is wrong, however. It is not the behaviour itself which needs to be tackled, but the underlying dynamic. Essentially, when the perception of the individual remains exclusive, and they function based only on their own perception of originality in a group, this easily creates an inflexible group dynamic. There is no chance of personal or common development.

Shared experience

When each individual joins the group with their personal authenticity and is receptive to the authentic originality of all the other group members, then a group identity is created. In this, the notion that only the existence of the singular unique individual, or 'I' is quickly replaced by an acknowledgement that other colleagues and their individual personalities also exist. In this way, the entirety develops its own unique authenticity. This shapes an awareness that every person creates a new reality.

By recognising each other's authenticity, an atmosphere comes into being which dispels the need to fight for the right of existence, but instead is accommodated by the group. The group becomes supportive and accepting. This means that the style you are accustomed to using, which allows people to get to know you - or not, can simply be set aside. There is no longer a need for bombastic displays of behaviour in an attempt to gain acceptance. Adopting such a framework means that the person who follows the group becomes more strongly motivated when he offers his real opinion. This leads to contexts developing where individuals are able to say: " there I can really be myself".

Polar force dynamic: transparency

Anyone introducing authenticity needs to have transparency in their environment; to work in a culture where one can really show themselves as they are and 'bare all'. This is not possible if the people working within the environment are not transparent about what they think and do. When they have a hidden agenda and do not show their true colours, there is a risk that an individual's sense of self-esteem will be compromised, together with the right of existence. The reverse is also true: anyone who does not show his true self from the outset, will encounter an environment which is not transparent. This makes perfect sense because colleagues do not entirely know the true nature of the person they are dealing with and, as a result, will not be entirely straightforward in their own behaviour.

Transparency

Description

Transparency amounts to being open about what you think. It involves expressing how you see yourself, your environment and the circumstances within which you are situated.

Everyone, in fact, through their intellect makes an assessment of the world around them and this is part of what determines attitude. Someone who is transparent shares this assessment and thereby explains their behaviour.

Conceptual confusion often occurs between this value and straightforwardness. However, they are not the same. Straightforwardness implies that you express how you feel, not how you think. You make yourself vulnerable by being open about what touches and impassions you, not by sharing your mental insight about yourself and your environment.

Translation in subconscious behaviour

For any number of people who exist, there is the same number of views of the world. Everyone has an image in their heads of how their environment appears, in their opinion, and mixes it with other criteria to determine how they should behave. In this way, each of us has a cerebral and personal image of reality, as a parallel world. It is not the actual reality as it really is, but is how we view it from our own unique dynamic.

Additionally, each of us is transparent, in our own way, regarding the analysis of this personal perception of our environment. People differ: one person is an open book and shares his vision and analysis effortlessly with others. Another person may be much more guarded and has learnt to keep his thoughts to himself. Others may seem open and transparent, but are not so, in the least. When everyone continues to base their behaviour on their own perception, complex systems result from this amalgam to see levels of agreement in sharing one's personal way of thinking ranging from not at all, to partially or totally.

The person with the open book mentality will be considered ill-mannered and coarse in a setting where transparency scarcely exists. But precisely because no-one responds to this transparency, this person will become even more acerbic. Should they meet someone with an identical dynamic who similarly bases their behaviour solely on their personal perception, they will both, in their openness, end up in a struggle to prove themselves to be absolutely right, taking their personal truth as the wager. The person with a closed approach is more likely to opt for a personal interpretation of their environment and runs the risk that their view of the workplace is completely unrealistic. When they allow this to determine their behaviour, they will face bewilderment from those around them. Quite clearly, they do not share this world and are influenced by their own. Transparency, in this case is far from being a reality. Situations occur where people present themselves as transparent, but retain a personal agenda that only grows larger. Energy is devoted to creating realities, which originally did not exist and never should have existed.

Shared experience

In a common perception, we assume that everyone, based on their own specific dynamic, is unconditionally open about what he or she thinks and does. This is not considered to be the best approach, but is used with the intention of improving the individual and the group. It is just by bringing these different worlds into contact with each other that a strong, unequivocal and common context comes into force. By showing oneself to be transparent in a group context and thus expressing personal goals, personal agenda, own intentions etc, they thereby state that they are open to creating an environment in which everyone can be nurtured by each other's view of themselves and the world. A common, cumulative vision comes into force, which is many times stronger than that of a single person. Everyone has an opportunity to check and improve their own insight. There is no need to always be regarded as being right about something or to conceal one's thoughts. In this setting, energy is not spent on masking thoughts. On the contrary, there is strong sense of surety, because nothing is hidden or held back.

For the company, this results in its presenting a confident face to the market and society. From a strong, unequivocal and transparent internal culture it will be transformed into an entity where people can conduct themselves openly with regard to their own agenda and intentions.

Polar force dynamic: straightforwardness

The polar force dynamic of transparency is authenticity. One who adopts a transparent stance and states sensitivities honestly, needs the environment to present itself in its basic form. This is the only way to feel secure about sharing their views of the reality and making intentions known. Those who do not show transparency will attract like-minded people. Thus, the individual will continue to work exclusively from a personal perspective of reality where, the validation of the unique right of existence for every other member of the group is absent.

The role of the core

The company core also takes responsibility here for guaranteeing the presence of a reciprocal nurturing dynamic. It asks each employee, at their own pace and within their own range of options, to acquire personal insight into the individual dynamic and to share this with everyone. The core provides the guidance and coaching for this process. By propagating this type of environment it becomes the norm to be transparent founded on one's own authenticity for the benefit of shared development. It creates the necessary sense of security required for each employee to really become part of the process of personal development.

This perception of polar force results in the ability of the organisation in question, to reveal its uniqueness in the market through open and clear communication from a strong and common realisation of the right of existence. As a consequence, it is ready to develop a profound relationship with clients and stakeholders being fully equipped to accept the challenge of deepening its originality and transparency even further.

Responsibility vs. understanding

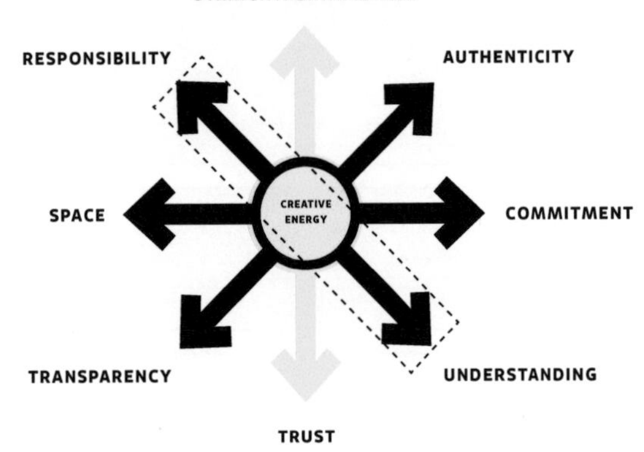

Responsibility

Description

Taking responsibility amounts to undertaking a task and completing it to the satisfaction of yourself and the group. This implies that others, entirely or partially, are exempt from this. But also that you are expected to justify the final result to your environment or the way in which it has been achieved. It is exactly this involvement with the environment, which leads to responsibility being linked to a certain amount of pressure. This value is usually associated with the specific job assignment and the task you are allocated in the organisation.

Translation in subconscious behaviour

Here, too, everyone exhibits a behaviour which is typified by his own perception. We naturally give either a generous amount or consciously little responsibility and strive to consolidate this individual dynamic. A person who takes a great deal of responsibility will, in a perception which is not shared, feel a great deal of pressure on his shoulders. He is, literally, on his own. If he succeeds, all well and good, but on the other hand, if he fails, he's left to carry the can. He will delegate little responsibility because by controlling the situation he must do everything to ensure that the task be completed as it should be. By contrast, anyone who naturally takes little responsibility prefers to keep himself out of the spotlight because he does not want to take the risk of being sacked.

In a situation where everyone is entrenched in a personal system of compromise, energy is used for self-preservation. There is no question of personal, let alone joint evolution. For the dyed-in-the-wool careerist, taking responsibility presents a perfect opportunity to make their way up the ladder. The result is a company environment where there is a trend of passing the buck and taking cover when things go pear-shaped: or just the reverse, where the creators of positive results are too numerous to count. Once again, it's clear that in a situation like this, we are alone - in a group!

Shared experience

It is important to create a group awareness where, first and foremost, it is clear that everyone, at their own level, is prepared to assume a certain degree of responsibility. This is specific to each assigned task. But to do this alone is insufficient in itself. It amounts to permitting the environment to consider this responsibility. The execution of each task immediately becomes a common responsibility. The person carrying out the task is no more than an extension of the group and the group supports the one responsible and motivates him or her to carry out the assignment to the best of their abilities. Along with the sense of responsibility, the way in which everyone carries out the joint undertaking is also important. This gives everyone an opportunity, through reciprocal understanding, to improve this value.

Subsequently, a context is created in which everyone is driven to do what he or she is required to do. No-one can retreat into the background or attempt to be top dog. Energy is not used negatively by aiming to be the first one across the finishing line to attain individual success, but instead it is aimed at supporting each employee in their assignment.

From this strong communal sense of responsibility awareness, a company is in a position to accurately assess its own responsibility towards its clients, markets and the society.

Polar force dynamic: understanding

It is important that anyone afforded responsibility should understand their environment. From their own level of competence they should take, in fact, no more than their fair share. Making this feasible for the environment to support and genuinely authorize them in this, it is important that they really make an effort to understand the situation. In this, they see the group interest as their own and, on this basis, are able to conduct themselves accordingly.

Because colleagues feel understood they will more readily delegate responsibility and really view the task in hand as the execution of what is essentially a communally felt responsibility. In this constellation, anyone who attempts to shirk responsibility will encounter incomprehension from their environment, because they are not shouldering the task the group has allocated to them.

Understanding

Description

Understanding implies the skill to create mental insight in your field, into yourself and the environment. In every job context you will need to summon your professional and social skills. In a technical field this concerns knowledge linked to your specific task. The more skills are polished and refined, the more efficient the work can be carried out. Socially this relates to delving into yourself and your environment. A better understanding of your own function and that of your surroundings provides a broader insight, promoting a more actively and intelligent direction of your own behaviour. In that respect, this value appeals to each individual's potential empathy.

Translation in subconscious behaviour

There are people who muster infinite understanding. They live with a sense of empathy for their surroundings and attempt to create a situation which suits everyone. Here we refer to the 'pleasers' who generate a sense of their own worth based on understanding. By contrast, there are also people who consider empathy a waste of time, so long as they themselves are understood. And there are those who constantly feel misunderstood. They are disappointed with the lack of understanding shown by their environment or in their inability to make themselves understood. Here we are using extreme examples by way of illustrating that this value is expressed in the most diverse behavioural nuances.

This value also narrows down from a uniquely individual perception to the search for similarly energy sapping status quos. For example, someone who puts all their energy into showing understanding will rub along well with someone who shows little understanding. In conversations, the latter fills the time by telling his story. The pleaser will feel valuable by demonstrating understanding, but will himself contribute little in terms of his own input. Ultimately, in this case we end up with one-way traffic in which only the other person's sense of isolated responsibility is acknowledged.

Another trap which often occurs in economic environments is that people with similar behaviour seek each other out. Reciprocal understanding consists of reacting against other subgroups of individuals whose behaviour they consider does not meet their group's norm. The group members seek the safety of the existing insight. And they fortify this by condemning the behaviour which deviates from their group. It is a system which gives individual truth additional value and nurture. Everyone remains in the safety of the consensus and does not evolve. Energy is devoted to finding allies in one's own conviction, not to nourishing one's own truth from a sense of empathy. This results in a clique mentality which sets groups against each other. They nurture their own truth from the cultivated incomprehension they have created with regard to other groups or the larger whole.

Shared experience

Real understanding is born of the science that everyone, including those you don't get along with very well, applies a specific personal approach to reality based on their own qualities and shortcomings to the reality around them, and expresses this through a certain type of behaviour. What is required is an openness in empathizing with this that is free from a judgemental attitude. Judgement of a certain behaviour is, after all, nothing more than a defensive reflex to justify one's own dynamic. In fact, experience has shown that the person with whom you feel least rapport, is often the one from whom you can learn the most in terms of evolving in your own job. If you were to make an effort to understand your colleague, this would improve the ability to better assess the situation and improve your own behaviour. Through this value a person can turn apparently difficult relationships or uncomfortable situations into opportunities for personal growth. This is because they are in a position to acquire insight into the added value of every perceived obstacle and to integrate this added value in personal development.

A keenly sensitive communal perception of understanding installs an educational company culture in which you give both yourself and others the chance to be bolstered by each other's strong plus points and talents. When everyone is able to interpret his own way of experiencing each situation and accept the attitude typical of the other person, a context arises where all individuals can benefit from each other's strength. Energy is no longer concentrated on showing that the personal dynamic is the only correct one but, on the contrary: it is devoted to understanding the other.

Groups with a strong communal sense of the need for understanding awareness will be in a position to intuitively assess supplier, market and society. They show themselves as flexible and able to move efficiently within the setting and show respect for the framework and dynamic of the broad environment. In this way, they immediately create a feeling of goodwill and lay the foundation for a sustainable relationship.

Polar force dynamic: responsibility

The polar force value for understanding is responsibility. Technically speaking anyone who creates understanding in their field is better able to take responsibility in their job.

In understanding one's colleagues, the individual will more effectively galvanize support in their responsibility. The better you appreciate how you and your colleagues function, the more successful you are likely to be in carrying out your responsibilities. In contrast, the one who lacks this quality is more likely to be left on their own. Logically speaking, if you do not rely on the efforts and strengths of everyone in order to take responsibility, there is little point in attempting it. The old adage rings true: 'Start alone, finish alone, in good times and in bad.'

The role of the core

Here, too, the company core sets the style by ushering in a culture that is aimed at individual and communal growth. Each employee is expressly asked, from an understanding of his own dynamics and those of his colleagues, to take the responsibility for developing himself and the entirety. Joining the company amounts to accepting this style of individual and communal evolution. Only through applying this kind of yardstick will the company install a culture where the energy-building collaboration described is feasible.

The creative energy generated from this polar force enables a company to be in a position, through its understanding of the client, society and market, to develop an increasing efficiency and vigour. It shoulders its responsibility unequivocally and purposefully but always does so empathetically. The outcome is that in every environment where the polar force operates, it will be better understood and will more forcefully validate the organisation in assuming its responsibility.

Space vs. commitment

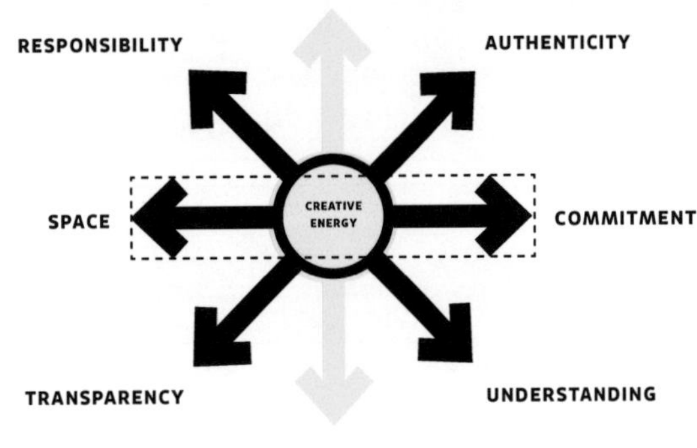

Space

Description

Space seems a strange entity in the midst of the values and it is probably more correct to call it spatial awareness. It denotes the physical space in which we function. Spatial awareness implies an understanding of the unique input an individual can provide in every situation. An individuals presence takes up a certain amount of space. We thereby claim a place where we can express and develop ourselves.

Space is regularly taken up with imposed responsibilities. The American President fills space wherever he goes. His spatial awareness is very expansive, in line with his office. By contrast, those without a roof over their heads in Rio are invisible by comparison. Their spatial awareness is very small. They allow themselves no space, thus their feeling of adding value is limited wherever they are.

Translation in subconscious behaviour

Depending on one's experience and conviction, each one of us makes a conscious or subconscious estimation of the added value of our input in our environment and claims the space accordingly. Some learn, wherever they are, to acquire significant space and make themselves very visible, whilst others claim much less space and, to an extent, hide themselves. Even though these examples have the same intrinsic value and concern for their environment, this is not identifiable in their individual spatial perception.

Individuals who operate only from their own personal dynamic, mainly use their energy to consolidate their own specific experience of this value. They create an island within the group and defend this versus the context within which they function. For example, a pushy colleague will do everything they can to acquire as much space as possible. Their environment perceives this as a heavy handed approach towards acquiring group space and reacts defensively towards it, which has the cumulative effect of making the pushy individual more over-bearing. The introverts around him choose a place where they can remain unnoticed. They remain silent hoping that they fade into the background and thereby add to their own limited spatial perception. These are but two small examples of the complications in the individual experience. Even though these two people would feel sure of their own purpose, neither of them would in fact occupy the space associated with the intrinsic value of what they contribute to the group. The spatial experience is limited because each reacts only according to their own truth. In such a situation, there is no individual or communal evolution.

Shared experience

Groups who develop a communal spatial awareness assume that everyone should get sufficient space to add their own value to that of the group. Each employee is guaranteed that he or she can acquire the space consistent with the energy they inject into the group. Such a premise serves as a type of safety net. But at the same time, this sends a signal to every employee, to be aware of their own dynamic in giving and receiving space and to share their related insights with their colleagues. This creates the communal and unequivocal understanding of the perception of this value. Thereby, everyone is able to calibrate their own behaviour and acquire the space they are due.

Both the assertive colleague and the introverted invisible person actively intervene in their own spatial perception via this dynamic. The first of these will perceive that they have the tendency to claim too much space, fearing that they may not be heard. Due to a greater insight into the group and themselves, they develop a inner restraint mechanism. Realising that, because they are more valued within their environment, they will direct their energy towards utilising space more efficiently. The second person aligned with his insights will similarly experience that it is worthwhile to be more visible. In this way, the individual action to claim space is matched by being assigned space by the group.

This creates the required flexibility to facilitate space creation for both community and individual development in a continuously evolving environment. This flexibility is necessary especially because the space around us is in continual flux. New colleagues join the company, someone goes on vacation, someone else is sick; these are all situations that demand a new balance of the space and whereby each individual will actively seek out their optimal position.

The balshy ones get the raise

In many companies, it is the person who utilises the most space and shouts the loudest about his value within the organisation that is heard more readily than the person with less spatial perception. It can be quite illuminating to look behind the facade of each employee to judge their real value, invite them to fill the space accordingly and to award the pay that corresponds to this.

Polar force dynamic: commitment

The polar force of space is commitment. Those who continue to operate from a position of taking and consolidating their own space are not connected to the group. They give no space and thereby negate the added value of the others in the group. However, when they really commit to joining the group they come to acknowledge that each person has earned his place. Correspondingly, those who do not dare to take space for themselves are considered to be uninterested, uncommitted and as a consequence will not be awarded space.

Commitment

Description

Commitment is a lasting value. It doesn't just appear out of nowhere, neither does it just vanish into thin air. It is a value that anchors people's solidarity. By consenting to share your own unique space with someone else, you thereby create a new shared space. Yet this action is often associated with the feeling that personal freedom is at stake and is partially sacrificed. In fact, you leave your comfort zone and in part, hand over your destiny to others to whom you are committed. Naturally, this brings with it a degree of uncertainty. It implies a level of surrender, wherein you have chosen to dive headlong into an unknown world to which you have, in a sense, pledged yourself.

Undertaking a commitment and the associated feeling of surrender is so compelling that it harks back to rituals, like marriage, for example. Gradually, the commitment has become a value tied to various rules and conditions. Thus, we can compare this to the norms of ensuring commitment within a marriage or employment contract. It becomes conditional and enforceable.

Translation of subconscious behaviour

Each person has his own way of committing within a group and attaching himself according to his standard. Often this goes no further than signing a contract and the promise to fulfil the associated demands. At times, when we retreat within ourselves and defend our own space, it is reasonable to expect that this commitment won't go beyond generalised limits.

The fear of losing ourselves in the group and giving up our freedom is perceived as a major barrier. This is often translated into behaviour where the energy is not completely focused on strengthening the community core with one's own qualities. The focus remains partially on the outside world with thoughts that possibly 'the grass is greener elsewhere'. One eye is kept on the outside world just in case there are better places to develop oneself. This results in a person with divided loyalties, standing with one foot in the company and the other in what is considered to be an escape to freedom. This lack of total commitment, albeit relatively minimal, denies out of hand any potential to unfurl any development present in oneself and the community. The concept of evolution is replaced by one that feeds anxieties.

Shared experience

Real management implies that you are emotionally and mentally completely focused on the group you are in. The feeling of perhaps being entangled and renouncing freedom is merely a symptom of fear and is not a translation of this form of surrender. Those who channel all their energy into the environment, discover community space and therefore a freedom that is many times greater than that of the lone individual. Those who commit in this way thereby ensure that the communal playing field of possibilities for everyone within the group is enlarged.

This has the effect of steering each individual via his insight determining the way he experiences this commitment. By sharing this awareness, mutual understanding is generated, leading to a deeper connection. The individual's input creates a clear communal awareness about this value. Groups that are completely focused on the group's interconnectivity develop an unknown strength that offers personal development and exploration of the world; the group and every member becomes stronger. Those who really commit to their specific environment will correspondingly discover new insights and stimuli thereby strengthening both the individual and the group perception. This develops the attitude that greener pastures can only be found in your own garden where you are firmly rooted. This paradox however, often has painful consequences for those who only partially engage themselves in an attempt to avoid missing out on opportunities in the world outside their group.

Rituals

Commitment doesn't always translate into a feeling of connectedness, but only in the legalised sense of the word. We all know the agreements and contracts which attempt to clearly and mentally define the scope of the commitment. The idea of surrendering and 'leaping' into the new environment is not present here. Thus, we can understand the importance of rituals including those contexts related to a sealing or announcing of a commitment. When finalising a contract and employing new people, it would be judicious to fix this aspect by borrowing an efficient simple and compelling ritual. Gathering everyone together for a simple toast to welcome the new staff member can be just the thing.

Polar force dynamic: space

The polar force value related to commitment is space. Those who make a commitment to another person allow a place for them in the newly created communal space; this force is two-directional and results in validating the added value of both parties. Those who are unable to commit themselves remain somewhat withdrawn from the area where they work. This, as a consequence, means that there is less space available for them. Those who do not receive a real sense of commitment from the environment are not strongly motivated to fully stake their claim; this has a knock-on effect so that in protecting themselves they demonstrate less commitment.

The role of the core

Once again, this requires that the company core takes the initiative. For benchmarking this dynamic, the core commits to developing a communal space in which everyone can put down roots by laying claims to their own space. This concept alters the individual's perspective. A feeling of safety is created wherein everyone is guaranteed the space due to them. At the same time, each employee is requested to fully embrace the implicit development dynamic as their own. This implies that through commitment and spatial perception, the individual should be constantly challenged by his environment. The assignment of this personal and communal development dynamic is an important part of the commitment contract that a ceo-organisation creates for its people.

Only in this way, can the part of the creative energy be aroused in the core to give everyone a clearer view, through group solidarity, of their individual input and the perception of these values. A workplace is created in which energy is not devoted to consolidating and protecting personal space, but instead to giving oneself and other colleagues, by means of a stable foundation, the space which is needed for personal and community development. The group awareness that has been created thus enables the company to commit to being unequivocal and trustworthy towards its customers and the community. From this mutually nurturing relationship, the company increases its space and thereby discovers the possibilities of repeatedly adding value for the people to whom it is committed, whenever required.

Chapter **ten** Sustainable growth strategies promote aura

In a word

The growth perspective enabling companies to evolve continuously in the coming decades will inextricably be linked to their ongoing deepening relationship with the world around them. This can be interpreted as growth strategies relating to the company's own staff, clients, public opinion and society as a whole. Organisations which invest in this now, can hope to develop a continuous and invigorating internal culture and an aura of authenticity and personal awareness.

Installing a new model for collaboration and assigning, experiencing and radiating personal core strength - doesn't that take a huge amount of time and money? Isn't that something which, for many companies, will only produce results in the long term? Isn't it logical that company directors, in this uncertain economic era will principally remain focused on short-term decisions and results? After all, they are not only responsible for the evolution of their organisation but also for today's success. These are the sorts of concerns that would be uppermost in the thoughts of a business manager. Certainly, in times of crisis it would appear more pressing to have a correct growth strategy in place to ensure that, at least, there's some money coming into the company on a daily basis.

Of course, - this is the reality. Anyone who doesn't succeed today in selling his products and services is hardly likely be interested in putting into practice high-flown visions for tomorrow's world. Nevertheless, the visionary CEO is well advised to use the leverage of fundamental changes, which really do prepare the company for the future. It is only the ones who change direction who will be in a position to spot today's warning signals of bankruptcy and convert them into a sustainable basis for tomorrow's success.

Company politics which are exclusively based on gut feeling and immediately tangible growth perspectives are susceptible to the rule of diminishing leadership, irrespective of the economic climate. Anyone who runs an enterprise in this way will, sooner or later, run headlong into the limits a constantly changing world presents. This can be traced throughout history, time and again. Structures and societies, which by their own perception seem to be reasonably successful, are not inclined to be involved in change that is in line within an evolving time framework. This is partly because this prefaces a period of introspection, of being challenged and facing difficult and turbulent times. A far cry from today's success. It is precisely the integration of this skill of the ongoing assessment of one's own culture that is of prime importance in attaining sustainable success. To take such a stance will engender a momentum that will spark ongoing innovation and evolution. Thus, an apparent slow-down can be converted into leadership. When you are able to achieve this, you are in a position to keep up with the world's increasing pace.

🔊 *"It is precisely the integration of the skill of ongoing assessment of one's own culture which is of prime importance in attaining sustainable success so that it sparks ongoing innovation and evolution."*

Thus, the essence of a genuine growth strategy is that you specify the conditions required to create a framework which makes permanent evolution and innovation possible. In the coming decades, this growth perspective will be strongly linked to a constantly deepening relationship with all the environments in which your company operates. A relationship implies a bond that is mutually beneficial on a material, emotional and intellectual level. The ceo-model describes a type of relationship where personal development and communal evolution are inseparable. This applies not only to the company's own employees, but equally to their clients, public opinion and society as a whole.

The internal growth strategy: permanent evolution and a strong radiance

This undertaking relates to the application of the ceo-dynamic in the internal company operation. The growth strategy laid down for the company implies a process which reverberates on all levels, wherein the company deliberates about internal organisation and includes the expertise of the HR management. Today, it is the first vital step from which stable relationships with the wider world outside your organisation can be developed.

By assigning personal core strength and experiencing the values in the ceo-model, the company, from a clear and homogenous centre, gives the employees the necessary impulse to exert themselves to their fullest, sure in the knowledge that they are evolving both at a personal and company level. Indeed, both the organisation and the individual feel driven to draw on their own creative talents and sense of responsibility to develop themselves and their environment in an active, involved and instructive way. The interpersonal tensions surpass their position in a rational (assignation) and emotional (experience) framework and are transformed into a real collaboration. The framework created converts clashes between employees into a beneficial and fertile exchange.

"The interpersonal tensions surpass their position in a rational (assignation) and emotional (experience) framework and are transformed into a real collaboration. The framework created converts clashes between employees into a beneficial and fertile exchange."

An organic pattern also materialises. Precisely because everyone retains their own set of values, no-one feels threatened. By acknowledging this personal evaluation, an openness is created which facilitates allegiance to the company core. It becomes accepted as a resource for the enhancement of the individual and the whole.

We thus develop the peripheral conditions to optimise individual potential, as well as that of the group in which the individual is active, within the modified prevailing mindset. This creates a setting and energy where opportunities are capitalised upon and setbacks are rationalised: a creative energy that is not counter-productive and obstructive but productive and innovative.

🔊 *"This creates a setting and energy where opportunities are capitalised and setbacks rationalised: energy that is not counter-productive and obstructive but productive and innovative. We call this force creative energy."*

More than ever, this becomes a dynamic process which is unending, and where everyone continues to reap the benefits because personal and collective potential is released. The whole group will continue to evolve and propel each participant towards a broader awareness, towards a more intense experience, towards more keenly felt insights about individual and shared qualities and strengths. The limitations each group imposes on itself are constantly transcended. This immediately implies that not only the experience but also the vision, mission and ambition will continue to become clearer. The stronger and more intense the internal experience, the clearer the organisational direction will become apparent to everyone who is a part of it. We arrive, as it were, in a stream of consciousness from where a strong integration of our thoughts, emotions and actions lead to a broader awareness. And that is the key purpose, after all. We're evolving.

"This unambiguity is visualized in an aura of authenticity. The company will become a bastion of its times, so to speak, for everyone who comes into contact with it, whether it be an employee or a consumer."

This analysis and the associated methodology not only results in a permanent internal evolution, it is also the key to enabling companies in the future to profile themselves as distinct, robust, and dynamic beacons in tomorrow's economy and society.

By cultivating creative energy, you can therefore ensure that the company, its individual value, or more precisely its self-esteem, is presented to the world with all its potential. Because it is able to pull together its employees around a strong core, it creates a continually growing and focused common awareness. From this position, it is able to conduct itself in line with its values and significance: in every contact, every communication and in every e-mail. This unambiguity is visualized in an aura of authenticity. The company will become a bastion of its times, so to speak, for everyone who comes into contact with it, whether it be an employee or a consumer.

External growth strategy: a ceo-organisation with charisma

The dynamism that a company extends to its employees encouraging them to collaborate, can also be employed in the other types of relationships that the company engages with: its own market, public opinion and the world at large.

From the developed core strength, the company becomes a vigorous organisation, unafraid of receiving input from its clients or wider social environments. The reflex will no longer come from exercising control on the market, but will be part of the way it is determined through its own authenticity. The organisation is aware that it will continue to be challenged in a positive sense through the impulses and signals it receives from its surroundings. By checking this against its own unequivocal culture, and on the basis of deciding what is positive, its value increases daily in all fields and in relation to all contacts.

"The organisation is aware that it will continue to be challenged in a positive sense through the impulses and signals it receives from its surroundings. By checking this against its own unequivocal culture, and on the basis of deciding what is positive, its value increases daily."

An organisation first profiles itself towards existing and potential clients - we could call it the market. We can speak here of a growth strategy for brands and enter the specialised world of marketing, advertising and customer relations management. Needless to say the natural aura, which an organisation develops through the implementation of the ceo-dynamics, leads to very strong added value for its external communication. The authenticity of the image created radiates onto the products and brands that it launches onto the market. The role of the communications agency is no longer to simply package the message so attractively that the consumer is seduced by it. The external appearance of the communication can never define its content. It has to disseminate the tactical or image messages to the world in a style and with a message that matches the company culture, in every aspect. Each message becomes an accurate illustration of the corporate communication or the brands' strength (image or product-communication). A correct interpretation of the brand authenticity enables people to recognise themselves in the company's approach and style, and consciously bond with it. This is the most efficient way of developing a lasting relationship with those who feel attracted to the brand. Moving towards the management of marketing and communication, the client and company become partners, such that each grows to become part of a mature relationship.

Broader still, is the communication and relationship with public opinion. It is no longer restricted to the clients, but also needs to embrace the wider communal context, where your company is active and where it might have a social and economic impact. This is a public relations skill. Those who organise their PR strategies based on insights into creative energy will enjoy a more efficient, open and direct interaction with the world based around the company. The media's role in this is crucial. Media training using one-fits-all type bibles to coach CEOs and spokesmen in how to handle their message and transmit it in function of the client, is outdated and no longer valid. The person whose communication is based upon open authenticity, thus revealing their strengths and weaknesses, clears the way to an adult and respectful relationship with the media. Again, self-confident people in the broader social arena will recognise themselves in this and feel attracted to the style and approach of the company.

Finally, there is still one last dimension that will become increasingly important for every department within the company if it wants to remain successful in the constantly evolving maelstrom in the coming decades. That is: to be mindful of the whole world in which we live and not view it as singular entities. It has become an inescapable fact that companies wishing to continue having an impact in a shrinking community cannot limit their relationships to a narrowly defined geographical area. In fact, in daily practice there are a growing number of alliances and networks developing between companies, cross border. The number of companies, large and small, selling their products and services on the other side of the world increase daily. No CEO can afford to turn a blind eye to this.

Those who want to get ahead must position themselves on the world stage; first and foremost by viewing the entire world as a potential market, but equally by developing relationships throughout the world with people and companies who have a similar market stance. Indeed, through a worldwide system of networks, new insights into your own company will be revealed. Currently, this field has not been clearly marked out as an area of expertise. We have therefore decided to come up with this term: 'global relations management'.

GROWTH STRATEGY TYPES

relationship with	application area
own employees	HRM
clients/potential	CRM/marketing and advertising
public opinion	PR
society	GRM (global relations management)

When we look at the ceo-organisation organigram, again from the perspective of these growth strategies, we notice that it views the market, public opinion and society as no more than an extension of itself. Its own employees are the ambassadors for the core energy, developed because they are closest to it. You could describe suppliers and partners in the same way. The next logical 'ring' is occupied by the personal market, or clients and potential clients. Then follows public opinion and the entire community. Due to its authenticity, the company becomes a magnet, interacting with people at all these levels via its philosophy of authenticity.

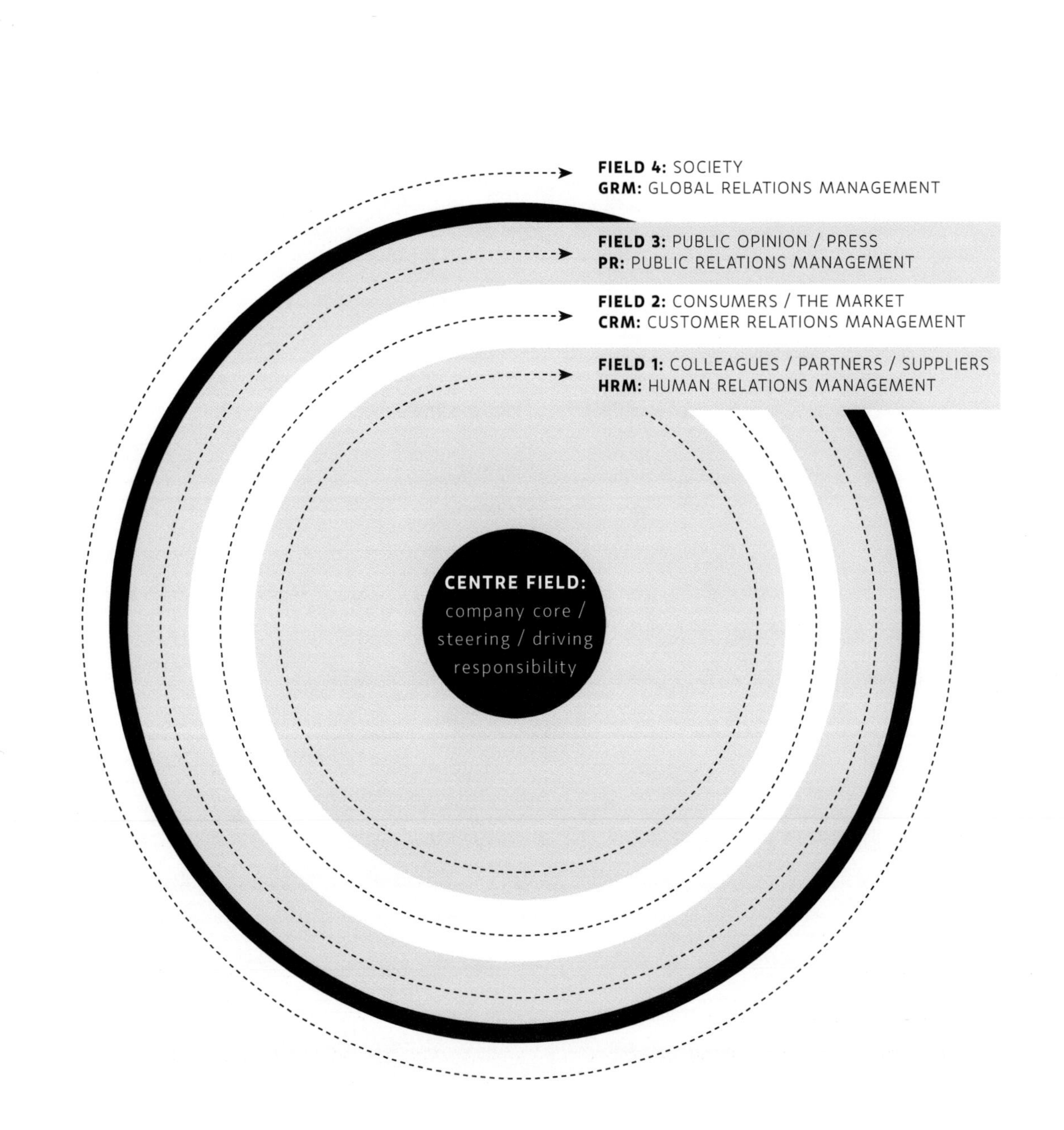
FIELD 4: SOCIETY
GRM: GLOBAL RELATIONS MANAGEMENT
FIELD 3: PUBLIC OPINION / PRESS
PR: PUBLIC RELATIONS MANAGEMENT
FIELD 2: CONSUMERS / THE MARKET
CRM: CUSTOMER RELATIONS MANAGEMENT
FIELD 1: COLLEAGUES / PARTNERS / SUPPLIERS
HRM: HUMAN RELATIONS MANAGEMENT
CENTRE FIELD:
company core / steering / driving responsibility

Communication: the content creates the form

As a communications expert you feel capable of delivering thorough, substantial and sustainable work when the opportunity arises. After a period in which communication and advertising was conceived as the elixir for extending mass manipulation, it's time for a major re-setting of the mould, so that it can assume a key role in economy and society. To make our vision on this clear, we often tell a story, which although it has some archetypal metaphors, it connects to the underlying truth. Here it is ...

Imagine that you have a communications agency and you are approached by a company with a beautiful small tree. The company in question says: "Out of all of the products, this one has the most potential. You should ensure that it achieves high visibility, is desired and is a money spinner." Naturally, as a conscientious advertiser you act with zeal. The little tree is placed in a shiny box, (since the consumer buys what glitters), and a beautiful bow is tied around it. The tree is placed amongst an array of other bling bling. But much to the disappointment of everyone, the tree goes totally unnoticed and unappreciated and everyone is unhappy. And the tree itself - well, that remains pretty, but small. It dies off after a while anyway, due to a lack of light, air and all the nutrients it needs to grow, things it can't possible get in its beautiful packaging.

Now consider for a moment that the advertiser acted otherwise and invited his customer to first look at the tree, checking its roots and stems, understanding what type of soil it best thrives in. Then it can be planted, sprayed and cared for so that it will grow to reach its potential and at a tempo that best suits it, into a beautiful tree. Now, because the advertising agency took advice about the tree and how best to care for it, it is able to explain with effortless conviction, not only how beautiful the tree already is but how much more beautiful it will become. He doesn't package up the tree, but knows so much about it that he can talk accurately, enthusiastically, and with all the appropriate nuances, about how it should might develop and grow. This success brings admiration and everyone comes to look upon the tree with respect and awe, savour its fruits and take pleasure in nurturing the new shoots that spring up, close by.

We like to draw a parallel in our professional life between communication and advertising, where the style can never prevail over the content, but where the content creates the style. In this sense, the packaging of a message is rather a translation of the strength of a company's strength (in corporate communications) or of a brand (in image or product advertising).

APPEARANCE
a thriving organisation, driven by creative energy, translated in correct and strong corporate and advertising communication

EXPERIENCE
your creative energy as a basis for a clear, strong and established company culture, positioned utilising clear and consistent internal communication

ASSIGN
in order to cultivate your creative energy assign the determinant forces to it

Chapter **eleven** Leadership: practicing power from the core

In a word

To lead a ceo-organisation firstly suggests that the company core behaves in a way that is consistent with the company values and dynamics. Moreover, it should not only act as the functional and organisational monitor, but also as cultural touchstone or reference point for the personal dynamics for every employee. To accomplish this, an organisation needs to be supported by a transparent and integrated communication structure with a HR department that is committed to personal coaching.

By opting for the ceo-dynamic, the incumbent management of a company immediately selects a conscious, intelligent and sensitive style of leadership. It represents the personification of the core of the organisation and is the benchmark that provides a reference point for each employee. Its first task involves consistently working with personal values and the related dynamic. It is only by a thorough integration of personal thoughts, feelings and actions that company managers can earn enough credibility to expect the same from their staff. They function as an unequivocal and strongly bonded core that gives direction and by the strength of their example provide the impulse for further development at a personal and company level. Anyone who wants to turn their company into a creative energy organisation needs to be able to defend their position through their own actions and be confident of their own capabilities.

Firstly, this requires a management culture that implements this within the company. It also needs to be committed to personal development, assessing and sharing personal and communal development, with the aim of firmly and clearly establishing the heart of the organisation. In practice, this amounts to each person with corporate responsibility at the director level, expressing their own truth in the knowledge that these ideas can be shared and improved by the truths of their co-workers, with whom they work at the core of the organisation. The result is that everyone engages in the cluster of the core strength with a sense of awareness, and not with the director leading from his own definition of correctness or hidden agenda.

A similar dynamic is built into the assignment phase of the growth strategy. Gathering around the table to dissect the vision, mission and value of the organisation, provides an opportunity for everyone to share their perceptions on the core identity. Each manager or corporate director has, after all, his own personal take on the mission, vision and values of the company he works for. This is based on his own experiences and convictions drawn from his current and former working environments. When everyone is given the option of becoming aware of this and takes part in a sharing of views, a mass of differently nuanced intentions and views surface about the project. Each participant obtains an understanding and broader view of the essence of the organisation and his own part in it. In this way, the seed of communal awareness germinates. A robust management core is created, capable of driving forward the entire structure in a clear, consistent and energetic style, based on an open and strongly bonded core.

From helicopter view to core insight

A frequently used metaphor when looking for mission, vision and values in companies is that of the helicopter view. In this, everyone is given the task of taking on a position affording an aerial view of the whole organisation and its operation. The assumption is that it is easier from this viewpoint to articulate the mission, vision and values, precisely because one has a good overview. This more classical approach clearly originates from our socio-cultural history, where heaven played its part in assigning missions. In the recent past, it was often the case that a mission was reserved for a select few. It was as if they were directed by God's will and, armed with a number of compelling values, had to convince the world, at all costs, of that personal vision. In this we have known clergy, prophets, presidents and, in all probability, a considerable number of CEOs. Perhaps it is time that we veered away from looking to find creative awareness outside ourselves but search in our individual core for the essence of our performance. This is why, for determining the core identity, we have not used a metaphor which hoists us up into the sky to gain an overview, but have delved more deeply into the heart of the organisation. This is precisely where we should search for the implicitly present, but not yet assigned strength of those involved.

The danger point however, lies in the assignment phase, where the process can degenerate into trench warfare. The strong personalities of each participant can shift the goal so that it becomes more about stamping one's individual right-mindedness onto the communal core identity. The question is not 'what should be mine' in this mission, vision and ambition but rather 'how can I, together with all those involved, best contribute to expressing what unites us'. In this, being mindful of the key premise is of vital importance.

Assigning the identity and values correctly and in concrete terms forms a strong mental foundation. Naturally, your organisation will not thereafter automatically be elevated to a blissful cloud of success. The company concept needs to be crystal clear, be maintained and be kept alive throughout the life of the organisation.

Tabula rasa?

It is seldom that, after completing the assignation course, the company identity is so radically altered that the organisation suddenly feels itself to be on shaky ground. This is certainly not the case. A ceo-session will not result in the company philosophy being re-written. This would be counter-productive and illogical. We recognise that you have built up something of value, be it as CEO, CFO, founder, employee or shareholder. This is why, after a ceo-session no-one has a sense of tabula rasa, as if an entirely new organisation has been born. It is certainly true that the ceo-session gives an undeniable boost to an organisation's evolution, precisely because it gives a more accurate and most especially, a communally supported image of your company's current potential and strength.

The first task of the member of staff responsible, following the assignation phase is to communicate this new style of collaboration to everyone. He or she should make clear what the mission, vision and values are and what precisely is expected of each member of staff. This immediately clarifies the boundaries of what is and what is not possible. These boundaries imply that anyone who automatically slides back into the familiar style of the old structure or uses the system so that via the enforced use of the central values only additional personal value is generated, will be taken to task by the company core. In fact, a safe environment needs to be created where people are able to operate in an environment of trust with each other.

The only commitment each person has in this kind of framework is to acknowledge their responsibility for their personal growth and that of their environment. It is therefore of critical importance that the established norms do not consist of a simple individual 'compliance' with the values, but are more about sharing the personal awareness surrounding it. Everyone is asked to take personal responsibility and to check his own perception against the central values. It is no longer sufficient to say 'I'm transparent, so it's OK'. It all boils down to being able to express what you understand by transparency and how you interpret the particular value in relation to your experiences in your daily behaviour.

Often a small manual is compiled in which this information is set out and where the specific significance of each value is disclosed. In a sense, these sum up the rules of play to which everyone needs to adhere, in order to make progress, both individually and communally. The organisation's internal communication structure will also be scrutinized. It is important that the possibilities for exchange at all levels within the company are maximised and made as efficient as possible. Ordinarily, people will find it difficult to share their own awareness with each other, if there is no means or opportunities to exchange this information. From the updated overview of the organisation provided by the centre-peripheral organigram, it is not only the most suitable meeting structure which will be considered. It is also worthwhile installing a new, simple and unambiguous meeting methodology which ensures that every decision is taken only after touching base with one's personal value perception with other colleagues within the organisation. Finally, one should consider which internal communication tools best provide a strong and integrated information flow. Here, too, new channels are opened to ensure that communication is not only functional but also value-driven, concrete and experience-focused.

Consistency - Practicing what you Preach

Also in its external behaviour the organisation needs to exhibit a style that is consistent with its explicit values. What you say only becomes important when you carry out the action. Thus, it is critically important that the person responsible leads by example, so your colleagues should witness that what you say is consistent with your own actions. If, for instance, one of the company values is 'transparency' and a decision has been taken not to communicate to the consumer that one of its products has a flaw, but you display behaviour which is contrary to this, then you can expect that your own employees will once again take the stance of a critical consumer rather than an enthusiastic employee. It's unrealistic to ask for conduct, which you yourself do not employ.

Certainly, such a cerebral component is only a first step. People also have to actually sense what is involved in order to feel they are part of the system. This is why it is crucial to create a solid support structure around the core for the new company culture via the installation of a value-driven methodology. To this end, an HRM policy would be put in place, aimed at coaching and guiding all employees. Through an internal training programme, everyone is given the chance to adopt the ceo-dynamic as their own. Through experience, all employees will be able to gain an understanding about their way of behaving and to share this with their colleagues. Everyone receives personal coaching and will be offered very simple and easy-to-use tools to put into practice the ceo-dynamics in their day-to-day tasks. As a result, tomorrow's company training programmes are not limited to sharpening the functional skills necessary to execute a certain task as it should be done. Instead, they increasingly relate to a more personal coaching process. Also, when new people are hired, specific assessments of their perception help each candidate to acquire a view of himself and of the manner in which the new backdrop functions.

In terms of management, the skills that are asked of a modern CEO are quite challenging. He or she is not only given the task of mapping out the assignment analytically, mentally and organisationally, but from now on, is also moving into the field of personality development - both personally and for the members of the team. Managers will only be able to tackle this when they appear as they really are: people of flesh and blood. This type of manager is averse to political power games and is straightforward, consistent and valuable to their approach to life. They are nourished and supported by the people who have enrolled in the exciting game of give and take.

This applies to the authority, which is their due, and which they spontaneously attract.

If you are keen to know more about the Roots & Rituals growth strategy for organisations, surf our website: cacao.eu or mail us on info@cacao.eu. Through our consultancy packages, we can provide specific advice and practical applicable methodology to also transform your company into a creative energy organisation.